AS THE

SPIRIT

WILLS

WRITTEN BY TRACEY ARMSTRONG

FOREWORD BY PASTOR PHILLIP MUNSEY

As The Spirit Wills
written by Tracey Armstrong

Lion Heart Publishing
P.O. Box 1117
Whittier, CA 90609-1117

Dedication

To my wife Nathalie who endured the late nights and early mornings of typing sounds, and for her encouragement through the times of writers' block, and many hours of research and editing. To my son Tristen Samuel and the other last day Supernaturalists who will receive the final call and deliver the final blow.

Acknowledgements

To Louis Orozco for hearing the voice of God which led to the writing of this book.
To Jerry Jensen for your seasoned wisdom.

About the Author

Tracey and Nathalie Armstrong are on the front line generation of "supernaturalists". He has traveled both nationally and internationally as a prophetic voice to his generation.

His boldness and powerful anointing touches the most hardened person, and brings repentance and change to people's lives everywhere. His wife Nathalie ministers along side him and operates under strong teaching and healing gifts. Tracey and Nathalie are committed to the local church as it moves into the last days with purpose and power.

C O N T E N T S

CONTENTS

FOREWORD

The future of the church has never rested on its rich, historical heritage. As important and necessary as our roots are, they assure us no future. The church has a future because of the zeal and imagination of young men like Tracey Armstrong, a man who has captured the unlimited potential of the Gifts of the Holy Spirit, and a desperate generation, craving something more than powerless promises and religious rhetoric!

The new millennium is one of the great experiences and Godly explosions in the Spirit. The passion of God to reach this world is coming to a dramatic realization. The Spirit of God will not return void... The Spirit wills... The time to see and sense the Gift and the Giver, is now!

Let Tracey Armstrong lead you with his zeal, innocence, and "Wreck-the-devil" faith!

If you are hungry for more...If you are looking to move from point zero to a place of world wide impact...This book is for you. The person who leads you has done just that.

Of all of the Preachers and Prophets our church has enjoyed...Tracey and Nathalie Armstrong are one of their favorites.

Pastor Phillip Munsey

The Life Church,
of South Orange County, California

Introduction

THE GIFTS OF THE SPIRIT

When I first became a Christian, my heart was to do whatever God had need of me to do. However, God knew the limitations of what I would and would not do for Him. But, two weeks into this new Christian experience I was watching a Christian television station and a man by the name of Benny Hinn was conducting a crusade in Germany. Thank God that I saw someone who believes in the power of the Holy Ghost and the fullness of the Word of God; not some old dry and dusty religious program with someone who looked so religious that it seemed as if they had a lemon in their mouth.

I watched as he was praying for a young girl of about five years old. Benny Hinn stuck his fingers in her ears and said, "In the Name of Jesus I command these ears to hear and to open." The first time he prayed, seemingly nothing happened. Then Benny Hinn said, "Everyone, stretch out your hands and pray." After praying, he began to snap his fingers, testing whether or not her ears were opened. Immediately the girl responded to the new world of sound. You could see on her face that something was happening through the intense emotional expressions.

I didn't understand what was going on other than the obvious that this girl was deaf, but now she could now hear. If I would have been watching an adult being prayed for I would have dismissed it as fake or mind control. Such intense emotions could not be manufactured by so young a child. I knew that this was real! I immediately knew in my heart that this favor wasn't only for Benny Hinn, but for every man and woman of God that would do whatever was asked of them from the Lord. At that instance I prayed, "God, if You can use that man, You can use me." You have to be determined to be used of God, and driven by the love that God has for His people. When I saw the awe on this young girl's face, I pondered the repercussions of such a miracle in the life of a little child, I knew that I was going to be used to change people's lives in a dramatic way. Think of the young man or young lady that you are going to pull from their wheelchair in the authority of Jesus. They will never again have to return to a life of bondage and control. Think of the lifelong witness of Jesus' resurrection they will have. Think of the change of purpose in their lives. God will use you to empower people to overcome the devil's limits. They will be resurrected so that they can accomplish their whole purpose.

At that time, I didn't realize, that the purpose of miracles was to witness of the resurrection of Jesus. Miracles will bring attention to Jesus quicker than coffee bars ever will. Jesus never sent us forth in His power to make a good cup of coffee to draw sinners into church so that they can get saved. I'm not saying throw out the coffee bars, but everything that we do to attract the world must have the presentation of the supernatural power of God. So many are coming to the Lord without being introduced to the supernatural power of God. How can anyone be expected to live above the natural realm if they have never been introduced to the supernatural?

The enemy is drawing this generation into a new

awareness of spirituality, causing them to question their purpose. Fox has come out with a new series of television shows that arouse the curiosity of spiritual power. The psychic hot lines are generating over 2 billion dollars a year. The church has been under the curse of the dark ages and the Holy Spirit has been working to restore the foundation of the church. We can now fulfill the Word of the Lord that the latter house shall have a greater glory then the former.

Christian gatherings (church) are not to get people saved; the purpose is to equip the Christians to do the work of God in their daily life. In the book of Acts the people came to the church after they were converted in the streets. That's why it is important for everyone to have a revelation of the moving of the Holy Ghost. From the businessman to the housewife! We must be anointed to take the power of God to the streets, out there where the people are.

Make the next sentence your prayer, "God, if You could use Smith Wigglesworth, John G. Lake, Kathryn Kuhlman, Maria Woodworth-Etter, Benny Hinn and Billy Graham, you can use me." God can use you; all you need is faith. Unbelief is the only thing that holds people back from operating in the gifts of God. You must have faith that God will use you. If you believe that God can speak to you and that you can hear His voice, you will hear His voice. God speaks to us much more than we believe to hear.

What we do is underestimate the desire of God to use us. So, when God says, "You can go a mile", people usually go half a mile; that's where most of us live. When I gave my life to Jesus I said "God, I am going to go beyond the limitations of my mind." If God says that you can go two miles then go two miles, don't allow mediocrity to short change you into living below your abilities.

So I stepped out, I kept stepping out in faith. It was very uncomfortable. Success begins when we will do the things that make us uncomfortable.

You are going to be uncomfortable if you want to operate in the gifts of God. He is not in your comfort zone. God will never embarrass you. He will never cause you to be ashamed, but he will always encourage you to go beyond your limitations. Sin brought limitation. There was no limitation until there was disobedience. We have to step out of our comfort-zone to touch uncomfortable people. God has removed the ceiling off of our limitation; you can grow in Him as much as you want to grow.

God gives what He has promised

The ultimate goal of Jesus wasn't to show off how much power He possessed, He came to be an example to us. He revealed the pattern in which we should walk and live. Live life to the fullest; go about doing good, cast out demons, and heal all that are oppressed of the devil. When the book of John is read, we shouldn't pattern our life after John or Peter but after Jesus. John and Peter didn't come as an example on how to live on earth. Jesus did! His ultimate purpose is that you and I are transformed into His image. God did not put a carrot on a stick and say, "Come on get the carrot" and every time we reach for it He yanks it back and says, "Sorry you can't have this." That would be false advertising.

Have you every gone to a fast food restaurant and while you were looking at the menu you see a picture of a juicy, delicious looking burger. The cheese is perfectly melted, with lettuce, onion and tomato. Quickly you order the triple deluxe double burger. Your mouth is watering, your taste buds are dancing and your stomach is humming. With great expectation you open the lid and to your amazement you find a disaster in a carton box. The wilted lettuce has slipped off the burger and is lying on the side, cheese is not melted and the patty feels like it's been in the refrigerator all morning. That's not like our God. He gives what He promises.

If you run hard after God, He will deliver the reward to you. It is not an easy life. It is a challenging life. But it's rewarding and adventurous.

When I was very young in the Lord I started operating in the gifts of the Holy Spirit. I started praying and seeking God three to four hours a day, praying and reading the Bible. I closed myself in my room and cut off all friends who had a negative influence on me. Later as I increased in strength, the Lord blessed me to lead many of them into the Kingdom of God. The Book of Acts became very real to me and I wanted the same experiences in my life. I noticed that everything supernatural happened outside the church walls, as they went about their daily life. So I started preaching on the street corners and on public buses; talking to everyone who would listen and bothering everyone that wouldn't. I don't know what I did wrong, whether it was my approach, maybe I was too aggressive, possibly it was the big Christian grin that was stuck on my face, all I knew was, people didn't get saved. That didn't bother me, I was in Amway, so I was used to hearing people say that they weren't interested. I just figured that most people didn't know what was good for them anyway.

No matter how many times you get rejected, never give up. Take advantage of that time to run to the Refuge. At this time I was just finding out about my Refuge. As I was walking around I would pray, "I am going to keep doing this until You show up." Remember the woman that persistently approached the Judge to answer her petition? After a while the Judge got so tired of hearing from her that he decided to give her what she asked for. This same thing will happen when you approach God persistently asking the Lord for His involvement in your life.

I Just Can't Stop

After riding the bus and having no results I would go back to my room. As Moses did I would remind God of His Word. I would say; "God, You promised signs following in Your Word, and You wrote it in the Book of Acts, I committed my life to the God of the Bible, You must be that God or else I will go out and find Him. If You cannot do what this book says, then You're a liar and I am not serving You." I was a foolish young man. I was so sick of the world and if this Jesus wasn't real, I didn't know what to do. I didn't want to prove Him wrong I wanted God to prove me wrong. The churches must prepare themselves for these young people to come. This generation is not looking for another fake religious Christian service; they want the real thing. This generation has the spirit of Elisha. They are crying out; "Where is the God of Elijah?" This is the generation that will bring in the new millennium, they are ready to tear down the altars of Baal in the world and in the church and rebuild the altar of the living God.

I don't think that God approved every thing that I said and did, but I do think that He liked my heart and determination. My mind was made up; it didn't matter to me how many people I had to preach to or pray for, somebody was going to get saved and/or healed. If one person gets healed that is going to be a life changing experience. If one person gets touched or saved, it won't matter how many people did not get saved. The price has been paid and a life is changed: It is worth all the persecution, all the spitting, and all the different things that happen to you while you are searching for that one ready person.

I remember one time when I drove up to Seattle to witness on the street in front of the Westlake Center, I would preach on a concrete structure across the street. As I finished preaching, I walked down to hand out tracts to people who were walking by. It was a very cold day and the people that were to meet me never showed up. That was the reason I had to preach and hand out the tracks. As I stretch out my to hand to hand a track to a man passing by, this gentleman started using all types of obscenities. This type of communication devastated my poor ears. As if this wasn't enough, I looked up to see his lips forming into a spout for saliva. Suddenly a putrid rocket of saliva leaves his mouth and heads toward my face. All I could think of was; please don't land on my face. By the mercies of God, the drop of rejection missed my face and landed on my friend's coat that I was wearing. Sorry, Scott.

You have to be ready for anything. If you call yourself a Christian, and you do not think that persecution is going to come, then you're fooling yourself and you're right where the devil wants you. Jesus was persecuted and so will His followers be persecuted. People are going to call you a fanatic. When you start to give them a word, they will resist. I remember when I started laying hands on people and they started getting touched by the power of God. Religious people immediately came and told me I couldn't be used in this way, because I was too young or God doesn't do that anymore. Someone even told me that if I expected God to move in my meetings and bible studies, I was putting God in a box. To say that God can't do something and not saying that God can do whatever, whenever, and however He wants is putting God in a box.

Go to the Word when this happens. It will save you a lot of trouble. Because of these voices, it took a while for me to listen to God because I let their words and accusations beat me down. Do not allow anyone to say to you that you can't operate in the Gifts of God. If it is the will of God and scriptural, you just keep on doing it and tell that person to mind what God is calling them to do. Protect your relationship with God and operate in His gifts.

The Gifts

There are three categories of gifts: the Gifts of Revelation, the Gifts of Power and thirdly the Gifts of Utterance. The Gifts of Revelation include the Word of Wisdom, the Word of Knowledge and Discerning of Spirits. The Gifts of Power include the Gift of Faith, the Gift of Healings and the workings of Miracles. The Gifts of Utterance include the Gift of Prophesy, the Gift of Tongues and the Gift of Interpretation of Tongues.

Please understand that the Holy Spirit works differently with each individual. Some of the ways He uses me may be different from the way He chooses to use you, depending on your personality. I pray that as you read this book, your understanding of the moving of the Holy Spirit will increase. It will result in a new excitement and enthusiasm for ministering to others. If one thing from this book can help you to help someone else, it is all worth it. There are no formulas to getting the Holy Spirit to move other than faith, trust and availability. Even if you have a little bit of faith, if He can trust you, look forward to some awesome adventures in God. Enjoy the Journey!

*"For us to experience
God's heart and
not be able
to distribute His
awesome glory
would be tormenting."*

Chapter One

KNOWING GOD

Daniel 11:32 *"but the people that do know their God shall be strong, and do exploits."*

In all cultures and religions there is a pursuit to know God, to know His thoughts, feelings, intentions, and plans. In Christianity this pursuit is a way of life. In the Old Testament, God made Himself known through His many names. Jehovah (self-Existent, Eternal, or Lord), many times you will find added to this name Jehovah attributes that describe God's character. Such as Jehovah-Jireh which means Lord God my provider, or Jehovah-Rapha which means Lord God my healer. The names of God are not to label or identify God as much as they are synonymous with His presence, His divine manifestation.

Experiencing God

It is also possible to know God through what we have experienced of Him. By what we have seen, heard, and handled. The Hebrew word for this type of knowing is 'yada', to know by experience, to know (a person carnally), or to be known. Daniel 11:32 "the people that know their God shall be strong and do exploits." The people yada their God.

As we grow in our knowledge of God, we are empowered for His use. We must take note of Exodus 6:3, God says that He was never known as Jehovah (Lord) to the patriarchy. Moses was the first to ask for and to receive the name of God. When the Lord appeared to Moses, He introduced Himself as the God of Abraham, Isaac, and Jacob. Moses wasn't satisfied with this introduction. The patriarchs were chosen to receive the promise and God was ready to fulfill His Word; therefore, He chose Moses as His deliverer. Moses asked the Lord, "Who should I say sent me, in whose name do I go in?" The Lord replies, "Say the I am who I am" which means, "I Exist who Exist."

In the Name of Jesus

Who's name will you go in? You can't go in the name of the God of Smith Wigglesworth, Kathryn Kuhlman, John G. Lake, or even of Paul. You must be prepared to go in the name of the God that you know, in the name of Jesus. We have people trying to do things in the name of other people's gods. We must remind ourselves of the tragic outcome of the seven sons of Sceva.

We must be able to preach, pray, and prophesy in the name of Jesus. When we can do this in the heart and confidence of the Lord, then will your name be on the "Watch out here comes the hit man" list of hell. God is interested in revealing Himself to us. Intimacy is not just knowing, but also being known. God is not only inter-ested in knowing us but also making Himself known to us. Abraham, Isaac and Jacob knew (yada) God as Almighty, because of their knowledge of the Almighty they were able to trust Him for the promise. When the Lord revealed Himself to Moses it revolutionized the way that all mankind would communicate with and relate to God. From this point on, man became an instrument of God's utterance and miracle-working power.

For us to experience God's heart and not be able to distribute His awesome glory would be tormenting. Could you imagine receiving the revelation that God wanted to deliver the children of Israel out of the hand of the Egyptians, and not having the power to utter the promise or to display the miracle working power? Revelation of a problem is worthless without the promise of hope or the power to rectify the problem. On the same note, the power of miracles and prophetic utterance is destructive without the heart of God.

Moses needed to experience the same emotional involvement as God. We also must be emotionally involved ourselves with what God desires to do in the lives of the people that He will send us to. While we seek to know God, our heart becomes entangled with His heart, we fall in love with Him and the things that are important to Him become important to us. Moses' relationship with God instantly changed, God not only appeared and spoke to him, but the Lord spoke and worked miracles through him. This was something that the children of Israel had never experienced. The time that Moses spent with the Lord developed from communication into communion.

Communion

Communion turns into love and love is the motivation of God. It's not enough to only know God as Creator, it's not enough to know Him as Savior; we must make Him Lord and seek to know Him as Lord.

John 14:13-15
"And whatever you ask in My name, that I will do, that the Father may be glorified in the Son. "If you ask anything in My name, I will do it. "If you love Me, keep My commandments." (NKJ)

The word love in v.15 in the Greek is the word agapao (ag-ap-ah'-o) which means to love in a social or moral sense. To love in a social sense is to seek out and to enjoy the company of someone. If you truly desire to know Jesus you must seek Him with all your heart.

Social Love

Although I love my wife more than any other person in the world, if I had to choose whether to spend time with Jesus or my wife, Jesus would be my choice. This type of love will cause you to abandon all for just one minute in His presence. This love will cause you to seem rude if you're on the phone or entertaining company. When the presence of the Holy Spirit enters into the room and He taps you on the shoulder because He feels the need to fellowship with you, you must hang up or excuse yourself quickly in order to share a few moments with Him. Unfortunately, most of us tend to abandon God and spend time with others that are demanding our attention. Seek to enjoy His company and watch what happens when He feels free to interrupt your life as He wills.

Moral Love

Moral love will never purposely hurt the one that it loves. There are many that tell God that they love Him, but then turn their back on Him when He calls. Love shall never purposely hurt, manipulate, or grieve. The Holy Spirit is drawing us into the realm of intimacy with Him to give us revelation.

Agapao love will do anything and everything to be with the one that it loves, and it will do nothing to offend the one that it loves. Vs.15 says, "If you love Me, keep My commandments." I believe that the phrase "keep My commandments" not just means to keep the laws or statutes of God. Commandment is the word **"entole"** (en-tol-ay') which means an "authoritative prescription." When we go to the doctor, we expect the doctor to be an authority on the human body. With this expectation, we trust that he will give us the proper prescription to heal our body. God is the authority on life and when we abandon all to be in His presence, He will give us His authoritative prescription. A prescription for dealing with any need or circumstance that may arise.

John 14:15-16
"If you love Me, keep My commandments. And I will pray the Father, and He will give you another Helper, that He may abide with you forever"-- (NKJ)

Vs.16 speaks of another Comforter, Helper, **parakletos** (par-ak'-lay-tos); an intercessor, counselor, or stand by. If the King James translators had translated this verse with the understanding that it is supposed to convey, it would read as the following:
    "If you seek Me with all of your heart, abandoning all to be with Me, doing nothing to hurt or grieve Me, then My Holy Spirit will speak to you My authoritative prescriptions. And I will pray to My Father and He will send the Holy Spirit to be someone who will stand by you. To celebrate when you want to celebrate, to be a prayer partner when you need a prayer partner, to be a friend to you when you're lonely, and to remind you of the image and likeness you were created after.

See and Hear

In **John 5:19, 30,** Jesus gives two keys to the secret of His supernatural life style. The first was that He only did what He saw the Father do. *"Then Jesus answered and said to them, "'Most assuredly, I say to you, the Son can do nothing of Himself, but what He sees the Father do; for whatever He does, the Son also does in like manner.'"* **(NKJ)**

When we put our visions and self-determined purposes away to allow the vision and prophetic revelation of the Father to manifest, we will be led by the Spirit and not by the flesh. You will fulfill the desires of the Father, accomplish the will of God. The second key is that Jesus' ears were attentive to the voice of the Father, always listening for the sweetness of His guiding voice. Jesus in His humanity realized that His decision making ability was limited, stating *"I can of mine own self do nothing: as I hear, I judge: and my judgment is just; because I seek not mine own will, but the will of the Father which hath sent me."* **(KJV)**

When we cast away our personal agenda to take on the mantle and Christ-likeness of our Lord and abandon all foolishness for the perfect will of God; we will see the deeds of God and do them, we will hear the voice of God and judge correctly.

When we live as "supernaturalists" we will walk as our perfect Example walked. Not just living a natural or normal life, because we as humans have limitations, but living supernatural lives because we serve in a super-natural kingdom, seeing, listening, handling and experiencing the things of God. For this reason, the Holy Spirit is with us to abide with us forever to help us live as supernaturalists.

John 16:12-15
"I have yet many things to say unto you, but ye cannot bear them now. Howbeit when he, the Spirit of truth, is come, he will guide you into all truth: for he shall not speak of himself; but whatsoever he shall hear, that shall he speak: and he will shew you things to come. He shall glorify me: for he shall receive of mine, and shall shew it unto you. All things that the Father hath are mine: therefore said I that he shall take of mine, and shall shew it unto you." **(KJV)**

Many believe that God is finished showing revelation and speaking to His people. Jesus spoke just the opposite; the Spirit is going to be with us forever revealing the plan and purpose of God. He will transform us into the very image and likeness of Christ.

I Want To Know You More

One day I asked the Lord how I could know Him in a greater way. He said that if I would pay the price and spend time with the Holy Spirit that it would happen. As the scripture says; the Holy Spirit will never speak of Himself, His purpose is to glorify Jesus.

2 Corinthians. 13:14
"The grace of the Lord Jesus Christ, and the love of God, and the communion of the Holy Ghost, be with you all. Amen." **(KJV)**

Our communion with the Holy Ghost leads us into greater understanding of the other two persons of the Godhead. At one point, I decided to schedule a date with God to meet with the Holy Spirit for half an hour a day. This time was not to include intercession, worship, reading, petition or thanksgiving. This time was only for communion. Just to see and listen. I found a private place where I would not be interrupted and set the time for 6:00pm every day. When I entered this room I would lock the door behind me and only speak five words for the whole halve hour; "Holy Spirit, I am here." The first few times I didn't see, hear, or feel anything or anybody. Around the third or fourth day, He came in a tangible way. In such a way that it felt as if I was standing in the middle of a room filled with gelatin. Although everything inside of me wanted to scream and shout with joy, I continued in silence. I started with my hands stretched forth to Heaven, but as the atmosphere filled with the glory of God I was forced to sit. He began to speak of things to come, things that He desired to do in the city that I lived in. And He spoke to me about my immediate family and future family.

Day after day we would meet. At first, it would take a few minutes for me to realize that He was there. After a while I couldn't even finish saying "Holy Spirit I am here" before His presence filled the room. Till this very day I have these intimate times with the Holy Spirit, but most of the time it is spontaneous. Sometimes He wakes me up in the middle of the night and shares secrets with me. Now we truly walk together on a daily basis and this all started with setting apart some time to listen for the voice of the Spirit. Stop talking so much and let the Holy Spirit talk to you and your life will never be the same.

The Teacher

As a result, my understanding of the Word of God increased, after all, I was meeting with the Author of the Bible! If you want revelation of the Word, just talk to the Author, He's eager to teach us. At times I could sense that He was more excited to give the revelation then I was to receive it. My prayers became fiery hot with the passion of the Holy Ghost. Then I started asking questions about the Father and the Son. Through the Bible, through circumstances and revelation He began to show me incredible truths. Revealing to me His Father heart and the heart of Jesus.

With such examples of character and goodness before me, I worked hard everyday to follow the pattern set before me.

I began to ask the Father at different occasions what His desire for a certain situation was or what Jesus would do at a specific moment. By receiving divine words of wisdom to help us walk through this life of pitfalls, we soon will be transformed into the image and likeness of Christ. We will return to our original state. This will enable us to possess the Promised Land and to take dominion.

In order to know God, we must commune with the Holy Spirit because He is our teacher and only He can bring all things into remembrance that Jesus said. The communion that we are discussing here is the word, **koinonia** [(koy-nohn-ee'-ah); partnership, (social) intercourse, communication, communion, or fellowship.] Communication with the Godhead is the ultimate goal. We desperately need to have conversation with and insight from each personality of the Godhead: through the help of the Holy Spirit. The Holy Spirit draws us closer to Jesus who, in turn, shows us the Father.

John 14:6-9
"Jesus saith unto him, '"I am the way, the truth, and the life: no man cometh unto the Father, but by me. If ye had known me, ye should have known my Father also: and from henceforth ye know him, and have seen him.'" Philip saith unto him, '"Lord, shew us the Father, and it

sufficeth us.'" Jesus saith unto him, "'Have I been so long time with you, and yet hast thou not known me, Philip? He that hath seen me hath seen the Father; and how sayest thou then, Shew us the Father?'" **(KJV)**

In v. 6-7 we get a better understanding of Jesus' desire for us to know Him and the Father. "If you know me then you know the Father." I must go on to say that since we didn't walk in the flesh with Jesus as the ones that He was speaking with in this passage, it is impossible for us to know Christ without communicating with the Holy Spirit and allowing Him to teach us.

I John 1:1-3
"That which was from the beginning, which we have heard, which we have seen with our eyes, which we have looked upon, and our hands have handled, of the Word of life; (For the life was manifested, and we have seen it, and bear witness, and shew unto you that eternal life, which was with the Father, and was manifested unto us;) That which we have seen and heard declare we unto you, that ye also may have fellowship with us: and truly our fellowship is with the Father, and with his Son Jesus Christ" **(KJV)**

Remember, the Hebrew word **yada** means: to know by seeing, hearing, or experiencing. Verse 1 gives us the understanding that the disciples (at least John) knew Jesus through His intimate experience.

When Nathalie and I first met, my interest in her was so strong that I would drive an hour to spend sometimes as little as 40 minutes with her and then drive back again. I remember times when I would call one of my friends just so I could talk about Nathalie. It seemed that every conversation turned into a time of praise about

Nathalie, I am sure that my friends were tired of hearing about her, but that didn't matter to me because I didn't get enough of talking about her. The more time that I spent with her, the more I would have to say. My communion with her took control of my conversations with others.

Losing Control

In the same way our communion with God will take control of our conversations. As we commune with the Holy Ghost, we can experience Jesus because the Holy Spirit loves Jesus so much that all He truly desires is to talk about Him. As we become closer to Jesus, all we can see is the Father because Jesus truly loves the Father.

Our lives will influence people because of what the Holy Spirit is showing us about the Father and the Son during our times of communion with Him. It will cause people to be drawn into the fellowship (koinonia) with the Father, Son, and the Holy Spirit.

This is the secret to walking in the realms of the supernatural! We are influenced by whom we associate with. It takes no effort to maintain a dead spiritual life style, but if you desire more than what you have now, then it will take you doing something that you have not done before and it may be uncomfortable. If we will pay the price to be in the presence of the Lord then we will be transformed into His image, what a glorious possibility!

Shocked By The Boldness

Peter and John on their way to the temple at the hour of prayer ran across a beggar at the entrance of the temple. They were drawn to this man crying for their assistance and were compelled to help. Peter, fixing his eyes on the man, said to him "I do not possess silver and gold, but what I do have I give to you: in the name of Jesus Christ the Nazarene-- walk!" Peter wasted no time on doubt and unbelief, but grabbed the man by the hand and pulled him to his feet. The man received his miracle! This opened a door for them to share the Gospel with all who knew the man who now was healed. While they were still sharing the good news, the temple guards seized Peter and John to deliver them to the religious leaders of that day. While under their interrogation, Peter, filled with the Holy Spirit, began to rebuke the leaders. They were so shocked by the boldness and confidence of Peter and John and with the miracle that was performed that they were speechless.

Acts 4:13-14
"Now when they saw the boldness of Peter and John, and perceived that they were uneducated and untrained men, they marveled. And they realized that they had been with Jesus. And seeing the man who had been healed standing with them, they could say nothing against it." **(NKJ)**

Imagine how these leaders felt as they looked upon Peter and John and realized that there was something familiar about these men, they considered their credentials and found that they were unlearned men. They wondered how these men could speak with so much boldness, how these unpolished and unrefined men could be used of God. It was so devastating to their religious minds that they were speechless. They could say nothing to refute the miracle. The boldness of these two men seemed familiar but they couldn't pin point the source. I can imagine that each time Peter spoke they would see a face flash before their eyes, the face of Jesus. They saw the same conviction of heart that Jesus had. They reasoned amongst themselves and could only accredit this boldness to the communion that they had with Jesus. While they were with Him, the image of Jesus was burned into their soul to the point that the scholars saw the resemblance.

We all can experience this transformation of soul and spirit when we commune with the Lord. His glory is going to burn so deep in us that our faces will shine, our lips will reveal the secrets of God, and our lives will be a divine connection between Heaven and Earth. Imagine the endless adventures we have ahead of us as we press toward the mark of the high calling: to be transformed into the image of God Almighty.

ADVENTURES IN GOD by John Graham Lake: Close to a South African city in which I was ministering, there were hills with outcroppings of rock- like a series of cliffs, one above another. I would go up into these hills to be alone and rest.

One day I observed a lady bringing a young child and setting him on one of the shelves above a small cliff. She left the child some food and water. It seemed a dangerous thing to do, since the child might fall and hurt himself. However, I observed that the child was crippled and could not move around.

After his mother left, I went over to him, laid my hands on him, and prayed. Immediately the child bounded off down the hill to catch his mother.

We must realize that Jesus didn't simply come to die so that we could be saved from the damnation of eternal hell, but that He also came to set the stage for world dominion and individual transformation. Christ is the mold for our transformation; Christ is the pattern for our lives, and through us He will establish the heavenly destiny of God in the earth.

People are being drawn to the love of God that resides within us. They will draw on the glory like the woman with the issue of blood. Drawing the virtue of God from the depth of our souls. The deeds of God will follow you: signs, wonders, and miracles will be a part of your life. Boldness will overpower you and will cause you to do outrageous things for the Kingdom of God. You will fall so in love with the Lord that your heart will leap when you hear His voice and you will be so compelled to share everything that you know about Him. This is what happened to Peter and John. After the miracle and the confrontation with Pharisees, the religious leaders rebuked them and told them not to preach in the name of Jesus.

Acts 4:19-20
"But Peter and John answered and said to them, '"Whether it is right in the sight of God to listen to you more than to God, you judge. For we cannot but speak the things which we have seen and heard.'"(NKJ)

When we are in the presence of the Holy Spirit we are drawn closer to Jesus, and as we grow closer to Jesus the Father is revealed to us. At the same time, the Holy Spirit is showing us things to come and speaking to us the authoritative prescription of the Lord. This is where we find our identity, seated in heavenly places. Don't listen to the voice of the religious "naysayers." And don't be confused by your own perspective. The Holy Spirit will teach you, encourage you out of your limitations, while leading you as a soldier of redemption. He will cause you to speak what you have seen in visions, dreams and the trials you have seen the Father bring you through. You will also speak of the things that you have heard from the Throne Room about the Kingdom, the schemes of the enemy, edification, exhortation, comfort and the things to come.

As The Spirit Wills

The Holy Spirit is the one who brings the revelation. He brings the manifestation. If you do not have communion with the Holy Spirit, the gifts will be hindered in your life. The Holy Spirit delivers the gifts according to His will, as Jesus determined, as the Father desires.

1 Corinthians 12:8-11
"for to one is given the word of wisdom through the Spirit, to another the word of knowledge through the same Spirit, to another faith by the same Spirit, to another gifts of healings by the same Spirit, to another the working of miracles, to another prophecy, to another discerning of spirits, to another different kinds of tongues, to another the interpretation of tongues. But one and the same Spirit works all these things, distributing to each one individually as He wills." **(NKJ)**

We have been misled to believe that we can use the gifts whenever, however, and for whatever reason we want. God divides to us the gifts of the Spirit as He determines for the reason He determines. The Holy Spirit gives to us the gifts that will work with our personality and our strengths. Very often a person will so desire a specific gift to the point that they will seek the Lord for the operation of that spiritual gift. Paul talked about coveting the different gifts. We can ask for the gifts of God to be distributed to us for God's use and glory.

The Holy Spirit My Senior Partner by Paul Yonggi Cho: The gifts are the possession of the Holy Spirit Himself. Since they are His, they cannot exist independently apart from Him. The gifts of the Holy Spirit can

by no means be used at a person's own will. Only the Holy Spirit can possess them absolutely and manifest them through believers in whom He abides.
The truth is not that man uses the gifts of the Holy Spirit. Rather the Holy Spirit, who occupies man and fills him, uses that person and manifests the gifts through him according to His own will, time and situation.

The Holy Spirit is distributing the gifts to individuals as He wills. God desires for every person to receive at least one of the gifts of the Spirit. It makes no difference what denomination you are involved with; God's gifts must go beyond denominational barriers. All we need to do is ask.

Hebrews 2:4
"God also bearing witness both with signs and wonders, with various miracles, and gifts of the Holy Spirit, according to His own will?" **(NKJ)**

The gifts of God are for the sole purpose of testifying to the resurrection of Jesus. The Gospel is God's power unto salvation and if we are to preach the good news, we must preach it with the power of the Holy Ghost. Displaying to the world the resurrection power of the Holy Ghost. The Gospel is not to be shared with only influential speech, but with demonstration.

Religion says that the gifts of God are dead. If the gifts are dead, then the Holy Ghost has left the earth. As long as He is here, His communication and manifestation is here. Traditionalists will tell you that we have matured beyond the gifts. If that were true, we would be sitting across the table from Jesus and the World would be saved.

Don't be ignorant, we have much work to do and we are going to need the Holy Spirit to get the job done.

Pastors, preachers, board members, please allow the Holy Ghost to take control of your services. You must stop thinking that you can lead your church into the last day move of God on your own. If the glory of the latter house is to be greater than the former house, we must stop throwing away the foundation that was laid, and start building on it. We can tell if the Holy Ghost has control of a life or a church by what is following the preaching. Is the Holy Spirit bearing witness in your life? The devil hates the man or woman who allows the Holy Spirit to bear witness in their life.

In these last days, the devil is opening his arsenal. False teachers, false prophets (psychics), false miracles are seen left and right. God is looking for soldiers that will rise up in the pure gifts of God that will confound the wise. We can't allow the devil to get an upper hand by drawing the world to his false, deceiving manifestations. The staff of God will consume the staff of Pharaoh. Could you imagine if God had sent Moses to Pharaoh without the power to back up the word of the Lord? He would have been laughed out of the palace. We would still be in Egypt. Just as Moses was empowered for his generation, just as Peter and Paul were empowered for their generation, we are anointed and empowered for this present time and generation.

Beware Of Religious Repetition

All we need to do is submit to the Holy Spirit and allow Him to use us as He wills. Giving God the permission to interrupt us while we are in line paying for our groceries in the grocery store. Ready to minister to the person behind the counter who has problems in his or her marriage. We need to listen for the still small voice as He whispers, "That man has a problem in his life and I want you to give him a message." The Lord will give you a word of knowledge or a prophetic word. He will give you insightful words of wisdom, discerning of Spirits, something to help that person. As He (the Holy Spirit) wills, allow Him to give you gifts. As He wills, allow God to use you for His glory and the furtherance of the Kingdom of God. Always be led by the Spirit and not by what you have done before.

Just because it worked the first time doesn't mean that it will work again. That is how religious traditions began and people were misled. In the early ministry of Moses, we saw him with God interceding for mercy for the people, communing with God, and asking for advice on how to lead God's people. But after being in the wilderness with the children of Israel for a while, Moses' heart grew cold towards the people that he at one time would have died for. Since they continued to go around in circles they found themselves again in the same place where there had been a drought. The first time, the people murmured and Moses pleaded on the behalf of the people to God, asking God to supply the need. The Lord commanded Moses to strike the rock with his rod. The rod is a symbol of the gift of God. It was one of the things that the Lord gave to him as a sign to all that God was with him.

That's why God has given us gifts of the Holy Spirit so that all will know that God is with us. Moses struck the rock and water gushed out to minister to the people. The gift used under the leading of the Holy Spirit is the only way to seeing the Rock minister to His people. Some are using the gift of God and hitting the Rock without the leading of the Holy Spirit, and God by His great mercy is still ministering to His people the water from the Rock. But these ministers will soon enough pay the price for their disobedience. The second time around in this land of Zin the people of Israel continued in their old ways. They chose the bondage of Egypt over the place that God was leading them through.

Numbers 20:6-12

"So Moses and Aaron went from the presence of the assembly to the door of the tabernacle of meeting, and they fell on their faces. And the glory of the LORD appeared to them. Then the LORD spoke to Moses, saying, '"Take the rod; you and your brother Aaron gather the congregation together. Speak to the rock before their eyes, and it will yield its water; thus you shall bring water for them out of the rock, and give drink to the congregation and their animals.'" So Moses took the rod from before the LORD as He commanded him. And Moses and Aaron gathered the congregation together before the rock; and he said to them, "Hear now, you rebels! Must we bring water for you out of this rock?'" Then Moses lifted his hand and struck the rock twice with his rod; and water came out abundantly, and the congregation and their animals drank. Then the LORD spoke to Moses and Aaron, "'Because you did not believe Me, to hallow Me in the eyes of the children of Israel, therefore you shall not bring this assembly into the land which I have given them.'" **(NKJ)**

Mercy Ministry

Moses was so aggravated with these people that he spoke to them instead of the rock in front of him. This is when he made his first mistake; he let his heart grow cold towards the people that he had to serve. Pass this test and you will last until we go to Heaven. God wanted to give them a new level of faith as they watched Moses speaking to the rock instead of hitting the rock. Moses gave in to a fit of rage and struck the rock twice and God granted the miracle to help His people. The

Lord will always choose and fulfill the greatest cause, which is to touch His people. The sad thing is that the Lord wanted to bring Moses into a new realm of being like Him. He desired to give him the ability to move God by speaking, this is something that the Lord has given you and I. We can move obstacles and mountains by the power of our words. For this reason, neither Moses nor Aaron were allowed to lead the children of God into the promised land. If we as leaders, can't go to the next level of whatever God desires for His people and us, then there is no way that we can lead the people of God to the next level spiritually, financially, or physically. God will raise up someone that is willing to change and grow.

A strong warning to all who operate in the gifts of the Spirit and desire to work the works of God; Never do what you think is right, do what you know the Lord is leading you to do. If you live by assumption and presumption you will find yourself in the same state of Moses and Aaron. They were not allowed to enter into the Promised Land!

"The things that no one will ever know that you do, are the things that give success in life."

Chapter Two

SANCTIFICATION

Daniel 11:32 *"but the people that do know their God shall be strong, and do exploits."*

Christian strength is equivalent to Christ-like character. In studying church history, we see numerous ministers of faith and power who, during their prime time of ministry, blazed the earth with the glory of God. But towards the end of their ministry, any flaws in their character came to the surface and often brought great shame to the Body of Christ and the name of Jesus.

All too familiar are the tragic reports of A.A. Alan with his drinking problem, and William Branham, who in the last days of his ministry got off course being misled to believe that he was Elijah. The lives of these men and others found themselves shipwrecked by the weakness of their humanity and lack of character. We shouldn't look down at the mistakes of these wonderful men of God who ministered with all sincerity, but learn from their experiences. I believe that God allowed these men to pave a road for our generation.

In my study, it was apparent that in each minister's life who experienced failure, there was a place in their lives where Godly character was deficit.

The Character Must Balance The Gift

If a person's character doesn't balance out their gift it can be very destructive to them and those around them. The Bible speaks of people who have a form of Godliness and deny the power of God. However, in these last days I have also seen people with the power of God but lack the soundness of Godliness.

Daniel 11:32 describes a people who have the strength to resist the works of the spirit of antichrist. Through intimate knowledge of God, strength is released into the heart of the believer. This is an unmovable and courageous strength: a strength that will not allow you to be walked on by the devil. This strength keeps you from doing anything contrary to the character of God. Most of the time we hear preachers teach from this scripture and totally leave out the fact that people must have strong character to handle the exploits of God. We have disregarded the fact that being strong is necessary for carrying a powerful anointing.

When Paul wrote a letter to Timothy, giving him instruction on how to pastor the churches in his territory, he listed in 1 Timothy 3 the requirements of church leadership. He described men of God with their families in order, along with their character in order. If these standards were truly applied today, sadly, many of our modern day church leaders would be asked to sit down until the character of Jesus was formed in them. Not saying that we can't do anything for God until we're completely perfect, but we should do our best to be like Jesus.

The gifts and callings of God are exciting, but just because you're anointed and have a gift, doesn't release you from the obligation of having your character being transformed into the heart and mind of God.

Paul never said to Timothy: don't neglect your gift and don't worry about your character. He put more importance on the character than he did on the gifts of God. Many ministers have thrown out the gifts of God because they were disappointed in certain people who never took the time to develop their character and only concentrated on the anointing and the gifts. In these last days, God is not going to allow us get away with being 'flaky, fly-by-night miracle workers'. He has placed a higher demand on our generation because of the example that we have had from the pioneers of the faith.

When I was first developing in the use of the gifts of the Spirit, I ran across some very serious character flaws in my life. Big red flags that jumped up in front of me to warn me of possible future troubles. Fortunately, I had a pastor that took the time to help when he saw these possible snags. He would always tell me; "character will take you further than your gifts." Exhorting words like these caused me to pray a prayer that every sincere person who desires to be used of God should consider praying. This was my prayer, "Father, don't allow me to be exalted or use these gifts until my character can handle it." For three years the prophetic anointing left, the healing anointing left, and character started to be formed.

Today, I thank God for those very difficult three years. I could have gone a long way on just the gifts. Most likely doors would have opened, but they only stay open through Christ-like character.

I Never Knew You

I once heard it said that it is the little things we do in private that are the things that count. The things that no one will ever know that you do are the things that give success in life. Spending time in prayer and reading the Word of God are two of these little things. As we spend time with God we receive a passionate inward transformation. When we read the Word we see the character of

God and who God wants us to become.

2 Corinthians 3:18
"But we all, with unveiled face, beholding as in a mirror the glory of the Lord, are being transformed into the same image from glory to glory, just as by the Spirit of the Lord." **(NKJ)**

The Word of God is our mirror. As we look into the glory of the Word, we are transformed into the likeness of Jesus. When Moses returned from receiving the Ten Commandments, having spent 40 days with God, his face was shining with the Glory of God. This same thing happens to us inwardly while we spend time with God. So when we walk into Heaven and behold the face of Jesus, He must be able to recognize Himself in us.

The Lord once gave me a word saying, "The world thinks that they can clone my creation, but I will cause confusion to come upon them as they try to build their tower of knowledge to achieve God-like status. In the days to come, I will show them what cloning truly is. The fall of man has put me into a place of not just being a Creator but also being a Regenerator, a Master Cloner. I will raise up a people that have the same spiritual DNA as my Son. I have cloned you from My very image and likeness. The devil and all of his sorcerers will not be able to imitate this. What is it for a man to reproduce what has already been made? What is it for him to take the temporal and regenerate the temporary? Only I can take of nothing and cause life to come about. I cause what is temporal to become eternal. I will cause what is natural to become supernatural. I will cause the carnal to become spiritual. For every cell of your being is pulsating with the glory of My image."

Matthew 7:22-23
"Many will say to Me in that day, "'Lord, Lord, have we not prophesied in Your name, cast out demons in Your name, and done many wonders in Your name?'" And then I will declare to them,"'I never knew you; depart from Me, you who practice lawlessness!'" **(NKJ)**

We can't afford to disregard the importance of Christ-likeness for the fame and applause of this world. Take the time for Christ-likeness to be formed in you so that when you walk up to Jesus you can recognize Him and He can recognize you. In the end all that matters is that you look like Jesus. Who do you want to be like? Who do you look like?

Practical Application

Discipline in seeking the Lord is a must for Christian character. In my personal routine I cover three important disciplines that helps my transformation into Christ-likeness continue to develop. I believe that Jesus was a professional of the highest degree. He did everything with the greatest of care. So I believe Jesus has the right to be called a pro. With this simple understanding in my mind, I thought of an incredibly easy acronym.

PRO

P is for praying everyday. Spending as much time in His presence as possible. Do not allow a day to go by without being in the presence of our Creator.
R is for reading everyday beyond your comfort-zone.
O is to remind you to obey everything that God asks of you. This one is hard for people who don't pray or read, but if you will discipline yourself to pray and read God's Word, then the obedience part will come much easier.

Fasting

By adding fasting to a PRO routine, your flesh will promptly come under the submission of the spirit-man within. Fasting is the quickest way to get rid of the old man and protect the spirit-man. You know that old man, the one that gets angered easily and loses control. He is the one that lusts after the things of the world. If you have been feeling dry and separated from God, most likely you are in desperate need for a fast. If you feel out of control in your flesh, fasting will bring your flesh to attention.

Fasting starves the addictive behaviors and ungodly appetites that would easily cause you to ship-wreck. When a person begins to fast, they become aware of the awesome power of the Holy Ghost present within them to transform them. Fasting brings victory over spiritual lethargy and complacency; it will fill your heart with revival.

Fasting is much more than just going without food. We must starve the craving of the flesh by not feeding its desires but feeding the spirit-man with spiritual food instead. If you go without eating and you don't replace the meals with prayer or reading it is only a diet. Fasting is not to lose weight. Nor is it a means for you to come up closer to God positionally, but it causes you to come close to God perceptively. Your ability to hear God is sharpened and you will tap into a source of Divine power that has always been available to you but you have not been able to draw from because of the control and negative influences of the sin nature. Many men of God, such as John G. Lake and William Branham, walked in power because of their life style of prayer and fasting. John G. Lake was a man of fasting and prayer. William Branham would fast and pray three days before each crusade. Jesus was empowered after fasting.

Luke 4:13-14
"Now when the devil had ended every temptation, he departed from Him until an opportune time. Then Jesus returned in the power of the Spirit to Galilee, and news of Him went out through all the surrounding region." (NKJ)

The Holy Ghost drove Jesus into the wilderness,where He fasted for 40 days, being full of the Spirit. After the temptation of the devil was completed for that season, He came out not only full of the Spirit, but empowered! Through fasting, Jesus received the strength to resist the devil and the power to change the world.

John 4:32-34
"But He said to them, "'I have food to eat of which you do not know.'" Therefore the disciples said to one another, "'Has anyone brought Him anything to eat?'" Jesus said to them, "'My food is to do the will of Him who sent Me, and to finish His work.'" (NKJ)

Jesus understood the purpose of fasting and sacrificed earthly food for the sake of doing the work of the Father. When we're fasting, God makes His will known and gives us the goods to get the job done.

Practical Instruction For Fasting

If you have never fasted, I would suggest starting off with missing one or two meals on the same day, substituting it with prayer and the Word. It is better to eat breakfast and fast your lunch and/or dinner. Next time, gradually increase the number of days. I would caution you not to fast thirty or forty days without having a confirmation from God to do so and a guarantee that you are physically healthy and fit. Before you start your fast, determine the length of time you will fast. Pray and establish goals for the fast. Ask God for the strength to endure and to complete the fast. When the set time is finished, thank God for the desired results of the fast.

Don't make it complicated. Some people expect an angel to stand at the end of their bed and wake them up every morning and give them the fresh word from heaven to solve their problems. Everything that we do as Christians is by faith. We started in faith, we must continue to live by faith. Don't change it now.

Many people get frustrated when they don't get their answer during the fast. I usually won't see the breakthrough until after the fast is completed. I learned that unless God leads me to continue the fast; it is best for me to finish it with thanksgiving on my lips, receiving the breakthrough by faith before it manifests. It has worked out well for me every time. Many of you may have a different result, but don't get uptight, just remember that God is moved by faith and not by works.

" The word is in
your mouth,
but the power
only comes
when you speak it. "

Chapter Three

AUTHORITY & POWER

John 1:12
"But as many as received him, to them gave he power to become the sons of God, even to them that believe on his name." **(KJV)**

He gave power to those who received Him. In this scripture the word power (**exocia**) means to have authority or delegated influence. He has given you and I the authority. This authority is given to us when we are born again. When you ask Jesus into your heart to be your Savior and Lord you receive the power to represent Jesus here on Earth, and the power to be transformed into a son of God. To receive Jesus is not a passive thing; it is intense. It is not just accepting Him into your life; it is a matter of taking hold of Him with all your might and every fiber in your soul.

Holding On

Holding on to Jesus is what causes the change in our lives. Some think that they can try God. There is no such thing as trying God. There is only getting a good grip and holding on. When you get a good grip on Jesus you can't help but be transformed. Metamorphosis is the result, just as a chameleon holds onto a rock or a branch and takes on the appearance of the object that it is cleaving to.

Don't miss the power in the scripture above. So many Christians are under circumstances and problems that they could overcome if they knew who they were. Let this identity become grounded deeply inside of you. Many Christians have a hard time relating themselves to Jesus as they read the Bible. Religion would want you to see yourselves as Peter; the one who denied Jesus, or doubting Thomas. I say no! There is a supernatural regeneration taking place in us as long as we hold unto Jesus.

Philippians 3:12
"Not that I have already attained, or am already perfected; but I press on, that I may lay hold of that for which Christ Jesus has also laid hold of me." **(NKJ)**

Paul states that he is not already perfect, not already the mature image of Christ, but he has determined that he will continue to push for that promise of being like Christ. Nothing can separate us from the love of God. If God is not going to let you go and you're not going to release Him, then the mark of the high call will be accomplished. The high calling to be like Jesus. He has grabbed a hold of me and I am trying to get as much of a grip on Him as I can, as was Paul's goal.

The Badge Of Authority

Exocia gives a Christian the same authority that a badge gives a police officer: delegated influence. The enemy exercises his power when given the opportunity, but he has no authority whatsoever. The devil desires to take your badge like he stole Adam's badge in the Garden of Eden, and just as many others have allowed him to do to them. If he has control over your body, control over your family, or over your finances; then its time to take it all back!

The devil should come to your home to steal, kill, and destroy. He cannot come into your life and just decide to take whatever he wants, because you have authority over him. *Example*: A police officer can stand in the middle of the street and stop the traffic with just a flash of his badge. The person that is walking or driving by will stop because they know that his badge represents authority. This is your position as a Christian; you are the one who has the delegated authority on earth.

Exocia gives the believer authority to tread upon serpents, scorpions and the entire kingdom of darkness. This is the same authority that we must use in order to stand morally and emotionally; it is the power to live a holy life as the Holy Spirit lives inside of us. That is the first portion of the double portion, the first anointing of the believer.

Acts 1:8
"But you shall receive power when the Holy Spirit has come upon you; and you shall be witnesses to Me in Jerusalem, and in all Judea and Samaria, and to the end of the earth." **(NKJ)**

The first point of contact was when He came to live in us, and He released **exocia** into our lives, which is the first portion of the anointing. At the point of contact when the Holy Spirit comes upon us there is a release of power.

For the second encounter, the key word is *upon*. The Spirit of God comes *upon* us for work and accomplishment. This is the power to destroy yokes and break burdens. The Greek word is **dunamis** (doo'-nam-is) miraculous power, force.

It is the power to be a witness to the resurrection of Jesus, to enforce the good works of God. Jesus is still showing Himself alive. As long as we accept the commission to be a witness for Jesus' sake, this power will be released to the believers of God. Watch out for religious people who tell you that miracles and the power of God are void and unnecessary. Anything that hinders the Gospel from going forth in the power and fullness that it is intended to go forth in is under the spirit of the anti-Christ. Just graciously walk away and pray for them. Religious spirits came out when Jesus started walking in miracle working power. Demons will be tormented when you walk in the room. So don't be surprised when persecution starts to come at you. Jesus was persecuted, so shall you be. If not, check your daily walk.

Acts 2:38-39
"Then Peter said to them, "'Repent, and let every one of you be baptized in the name of Jesus Christ for the remission of sins; and you shall receive the gift of the Holy Spirit. For the promise is to you and to your children, and to all who are afar off, as many as the Lord our God will call.'" **(NKJ)**

Everyone is called and everyone is called to be baptized and receive the gift of the Holy Spirit. You are called by God to be empowered with His resurrection power, regardless of your denominational or social background. Every Christian is to be a witness of the resurrection of Jesus.

Magnum

To give you an understanding of the second portion of the anointing (dunamis), let's go back to the analogy of the police officer. If the fact that this one officer represents thousands of other officers and judicial officers doesn't stop an offender or criminal, and he chooses to ignore the authority and instructions of the officer, the officer must judge whether or not deadly force is needed. There are two reasons for deadly force, if the officers' life is in danger or if the public is in danger. If deadly force is needed, then the officer has a gun. For the sake of our analogy we will call this gun dunamis. The force behind this gun will help him keep the peace.

If the devil challenges our authority and tries to ignore the many other 'officers' on our side, we are forced to use deadly force. The devil is a dangerous criminal and cannot be ignored, so stop trying to make treaties with him and destroy his works in Jesus' Name!

Authority Through The Word

The Word of God is a wonderful weapon of spiritual warfare and power. The best example of this is found in Luke 4. It is the story of when Jesus was confronted by the devil regarding His identity as the Son of God. In chapter 3:22, the Holy Spirit descended upon Jesus and the voice of God comes from heaven declaring, "You are My beloved Son; in You I am well pleased." In chapter 4, the Holy Spirit led Jesus into the wilderness.

Just a side note, some of you that feel dry, as if you are in the wilderness, it could be that God is setting you up for a promotion! Look through the Bible and see what happened to the people who were driven into the wilderness by God. They were promoted shortly afterward. Red dot yourself during these times checking your emotional and character growth along the way.

While Jesus was in the wilderness He became subject to several temptations. Each of them strategically plotted out to crush the identity of Jesus as the Son of God. The first was when Jesus had just finished His 40 day fast. The devil tempted Him to turn some nearby stones into bread. Jesus resisted the temptation by proclaiming the written Word and overcame the temptation.

Selfish Motivation Test

It was not wrong for Jesus to use His miracle working power. But it would have been wrong for Him to use it at the devil's command. It was a test of using the power of God for selfish gains. As you develop in your spiritual gifts, watch out for this temptation. So Jesus answered him, saying, "It is written, 'Man shall not live by bread alone, but by every word of God." This was an awesome use of the **logos** Word (reasoned speech). Jesus had the Word written in His heart so He was able to reply to the devil through reason.

Challenged For Authority

The devil was not willing to give up at this point so he took Jesus to a high mountain, then he showed Him all the kingdoms of the world in a moment of time. He could not have shown Jesus all the kingdoms from one vantage point. I believe that the devil showed Jesus a form of his power, the glory of dominion that he stole from Adam. The devil had the audacity to say to Jesus "All this authority I will give You, and their glory; for this has been delivered to me, and I give it to whomever I wish. Therefore, if You will worship before me, all will be Yours." Jesus, knowing that the devil had no authority over Him answered and said to him; "Get behind Me, Satan! For it is written, You shall worship the Lord your God, and Him only you shall serve." Again, Jesus had returned a bruising blow to the devil with the **logos** (the reasoned speech).

This is the test that Adam failed. It might be obvious to us that if we worship the devil, we will lose our authority, but when we give into sin, we are doing just that.

The Vain Glory Test

In Genesis it says that the snake was the most cunning creature in the garden. Well, he is still cunning. Thank God that we are not ignorant of his devices. He came back to Jesus with his last and hardest blow. He brought Jesus to Jerusalem, set Him on the pinnacle of the temple, and said to Him, "If You are the Son of God, (again challenging his identity) throw Yourself down from here. For it is written: 'He shall give His angels charge over You, to keep You, and, In their hands they shall bear you up, lest you dash your foot against a stone." This one just could have thrown Jesus for a loop. Just think about this temptation: It was Jesus' greatest desire to glorify the Father, what better way than to get the city of Jerusalem saved in one day. Maybe it was the day that everyone went to the market and if he had plunged Himself down, the whole city would have seen the angels save Him from certain death.

The devil is completely perverted; he took the Word of God and tried to manipulate it to his own advantage. The devil will try to tempt you by getting you to flaunt your gifts and so cause vainglory to come to you. You might hope that man would recognize you as a man or woman of God. Don't fall for this trap! I believe Jesus nearly cut off the devil's head with this next answer, was such a severe blow that the enemy had to leave. Jesus answering and said to him, "It has been said, 'You shall not tempt the Lord your God." You may have read this and do not understand the power of it.

Enough Is Enough

Each time the devil came to attack Jesus, the Lord used the **logos**, the written, reasoned word to combat the enemy. This final time the enemy decided to use the written Word. But Jesus came back at him with the **rhema**, an uttered word. It has been said implies that Jesus heard something said. The Father in heaven must have seen the perverted devil trying to trick the Son of Man by using the Word of God against Him. I believe the Father sat up in His throne, stretched forth His finger and said: "Enough is enough!" "You shall not tempt the Lord your God." Jesus in His time of need needed something to help Him through this temptation. Jesus fought and fought with the **logos** until He heard the voice of God, which brought the **rhema**. When He heard the **rhema** word it caused faith to rise up within Him.

Romans 10:17
"So then faith comes by hearing, and hearing by the word of God." **(NKJ)**

After faith rose in His heart, the devil couldn't stick around. The devil can't stand faith; that's why he hopes that Christians won't hear the voice of God. Jesus received such victory in the wilderness through the **logos** and **rhema** word that He walked out of the wilderness empowered by the Holy Ghost. He went in led by the Spirit full of the Spirit and came out with such power that everyone in Galilee heard about it including the demons of hell!

Come on Christians! The Word is near you, even in your mouth, but the power only comes when you speak it. Speak the Word!

Authority From The Anointing

God wants to anoint us with the Holy Ghost and with power just as He anointed Jesus. To be anointed means to be smeared or rubbed with oil. The anointing on us will enable us to accomplish in God what we couldn't do without Him. God's super on our natural. Now I just want to clear up some of the misconceptions people sometimes have concerning the anointing or anointed individuals. Many people believe that the anointing will take care of any weakness in their souls and even cause their character to change instantly. This is a false assumption: soul and character changes only come through the renewing of the mind. Whether it's through trials or study of the Word of God: exchanging your old thoughts for God's thoughts.

Anointing, Or A Good Show?

Please don't confuse the anointing with a good show. The anointing brings results. It's not enough to appear to be anointed we must be anointed. The anointing is for the purpose of doing work in the Kingdom of God. Do yourself a favor; don't ask for the anointing if you're not planning to do anything with the power that comes with being anointed.

The anointing is an amplifier for the gifts of God. It is life to dead bodies and dead spirits. The anointing is the power that breaks the yokes of bondage. When a person is approved of God, the Holy Spirit will be smeared all over them to lead, teach, and empower them.

Acts 10:38
"how God anointed Jesus of Nazareth with the Holy Spirit and with power, who went about doing good and healing all who were oppressed by the devil, for God was with Him." **(NKJ)**

When the Holy Spirit comes upon someone, the anointing is a result. Please don't get confused between the Holy Spirit and the anointing. The Holy Spirit is God and the anointing is the favor of God. When you're smeared by the Holy Spirit, He walks with you, leads you, and talks to you. When you're anointed with power, the Holy Spirit destroys yokes for you and through you.

Smith Wigglesworth was so anointed that sometimes the people around him would begin to cry out for help because the conviction of the Holy Spirit would come so strong upon them that they thought that they felt like they were going to die. People still get healed while watching the videotapes of Kathryn Kuhlman because God anointed her with the Holy Ghost and power. She may have past on to glory, but the Holy Ghost is still working in the earth. Elisha's bones were so anointed that when some men threw a dead man on his bones the man came back to life.

Charles Finney was so anointed that, one day he went to a sewing factory to look around and a revival broke out in this mill. Autobiography by Charles G. Finney: "I went into the factory, to look through it. As I went through, I observed there was a good deal of agitation among those who were busy at their looms, and their mules, and other implements of work. On passing through one of the apartments, where a great number of young women were attending to their weaving, I observed a couple of them eyeing me, and speaking very earnestly to each other; and I could see that they were a good deal agitated, although they both laughed. I went slowly toward them. They saw me coming, and were evidently much excited. One of them was trying to mend a broken thread, and I observed that her hands trembled so that she could not mend it. I approached slowly, looking on each side at the machinery, as I passed; but observed that this girl grew more and more agitated, and could not proceed with her work. When I came within eight or ten feet of her, I looked solemnly at her. She observed it, and was quite overcome, and sunk down, and burst into tears. The impression caught almost like powder and in a few moments nearly all in the room were in tears. This spread through the factory. The owner of the establishment, "Stop the mill, and let's attend to religion; for it is more important that our souls should be saved than that this factory run." The gate was immediately shut down, and the factory stopped; The revival went through the mill with astonishing power, and in the course of a few days nearly all in the mill were hopefully converted."

Miracles will follow the person with the anointing. Jesus went about doing good and healing all that were under the dominion of the devil. The anointing is proof that God is with you.

Isaiah 10:27
"It shall come to pass in that day that his burden will be taken away from your shoulder, and his yoke from your neck, and the yoke will be destroyed because of the anointing oil." **(NKJ)**

The anointing is a vital part of the ministry of a Christian. Where the Spirit of the Lord is, there is freedom. Where the Holy Spirit is, there is the burden removing, yoke of the devil busting, power of God. If you want the glory of God, make sure that God is with you. If God is with you, then His anointing will be on you.

"The prophetic promise
of a better tomorrow will
cause a hunger to
arise in even
the dullest of souls."

Chapter Four

THE GIFTS OF REVELATION

1 Corinthians 12:3-7
"Therefore, I make known to you that no one speaking by the Spirit of God calls Jesus accursed, and no one can say that Jesus is Lord except by the Holy Spirit. There are diversities of gifts, but the same Spirit. There are differences of ministries, but the same Lord. And there are diversities of activities, but it is the same God who works all in all. But the manifestation of the Spirit is given to each one for the profit of all:" **(NKJ)**

The first thing Paul says in verse 4 is, "There are diversities of gifts, but the same Spirit." The Holy Spirit delivers all the gifts of God to us. The Holy Spirit delivers the word of knowledge, word of wisdom and all the other gifts of the Spirit. For this reason, we should rely completely on His leading and instruction for the use of the gifts of the Spirit.

Inspired Revelation vs. Mental Reasoning
The gifts of revelation can be difficult to recognize because when they are received they must work past the "filter" of our human reasoning. Although they work within the realm of mental reason, they do not need to be

submitted to mental reason. Often impressions or flashes of insight are interpreted as being the imagination. We must train our minds to differentiate between our mind and the mind of Christ. The difficult thing is to separate the inspired revelation from mental reasoning. The line is so fine that we could easily say that revelation initiated by God could be vain imagination and vice-versa. The key to deciphering the difference is discernment and understanding, which we receive through the Word, prayer, and the anointing.

In the book, "God's Generals" a collection of historical facts of Men and Women of God gathered by Roberts Liardon, we find insight into William Branham's early years and how his spiritual gift progressed. When William Branham first started operating in the gift of revelation, he didn't immediately understand every vision that he saw. Sometimes he would have to leave the room where he was praying for someone in order to seek the Lord for understanding. He would then return and release the Word and ministry. After some time of going through this type of development, his confidence in the gift increased to the point that he could meet someone for the first time and the Lord could give revelation so distinct that it would shock those receiving the ministry. He frequently called out names, addresses, and illnesses.

It is very important not to become discouraged during this time of development of the gifts of revelation. I believe that we can all step into this realm of power and revelation if we are willing to become trustworthy to the Holy Spirit. Making mistakes and missing the mark are all part of developing in the use of the gifts of revelation. One thing is for sure; you can't miss it if you never step out in faith, nor can you be fruitful in the Kingdom of God if you never take the first step. All of the gifts are developed through the reason of use, the more you use them the more God trusts you.

Give Freely

The spiritual law of 'give and it shall be given to you', truly applies here. Why would the Lord entrust someone with the ability to receive names and addresses if that person won't be faithful with revelation of lesser distinction? As you freely give the gift of God out, God will find you faithful with little and will give you more. Healing, love, grace and power are all to be given freely. What good is a gift if it is not given out?

Matthew 10:8
"Heal the sick, cleanse the lepers, raise the dead, cast out demons. Freely you have received freely give." **(NKJ)**

Trust the Holy Spirit to teach you and train you personally. If He can train you He can also trust you. The whole relationship between God, you, and His gifts is about being able to trust one another and that's why God needs to be able to trust you to give away what He has given you. It's the same with money, power, grace, and mercy etc.; give and it shall be given to you.

Your Spirit Man

As children of God, our intuition or instantaneous comprehension works within the realms of the spirit, controlled by our spirit man. The world calls it the subconscious mind because their spirits are dead to God. Their soul is in complete control of their lives. The Christian believer's soul should be submitted to the spirit man and the demand of Holy Spirit. Our soul, which is that instrument through which our intuition manifests in the natural realm, is submitted to our spirit man who is joined to the Holy Spirit. Since we are joined to the Spirit of God and we do have the mind of Christ, most of the impressions and images we receive shouldn't be mentally inspired but God inspired. We are then able to walk as supernatural people.

At times, when God is inspiring something within us, to our minds it will be so far-fetched that we choose not to believe that it will work. The best thing to do is to ask the Lord if these images originated from whether it is demonic or mentally inspired. Don't be hesitant to pray for God to confirm. If it's from God; he'll let you know. Many inventions may very well be waiting on a Christian to take initiative on a God inspired idea. It's time for us to set the pace and the standard in this life, and the gifts of the Lord will help us do this.

The Godhead

For too long we have underestimated what God has entrusted us with. The following verse, verse 5, starts to categorize each person of the Godhead and their duties. Paul says that there are diversities of gifts but the same Spirit and diversities of administration but the same Lord. Who is our Lord? Of course, it is Jesus.

Then Paul continues by saying there are diversities of operations, but the same God. Let's call God the operator. Then he says the manifestation is given to each child of God, but the manifestation comes by the Spirit of God. Here we have every single person of the Godhead represented. The Father, who is in charge of operations, is the one that is saying, "I desire light." The Father is the operator, the chief who initiates the plan. Now Jesus is the next in line and He being the administrator, draws up the blue prints and says light should be bright, it should give heat and illumination in the night. So Jesus organizes and gives a job description to the command, how everything should look and function. The

Father says I want light and Jesus says I want light to look like this. Jesus does not manifest the light nor does the Father. Who brings the manifested light? The Holy Spirit! So we see every single person of the Godhead is involved.

Greater Works

This is where you come into play, how you become involved. John 14:12 says, "He that believes on me..." The one that believes on Me shall do these works also and then He goes on to say, "and greater works than these shall he do because I go to the Father." Jesus was about to go on to the Father and delegated His work unto us. The only qualification He states is to believe on Him and we shall do the same works and greater works because He went on to be with the Father.

In verse 13, He says, " If you ask anything in my name I shall do it." Now our God is not a man that He should lie. If He says it, then He means it. Verse 15 He (the Holy Spirit) dwells with you and shall be in you.

Verse 18-19 The world shall see Jesus no more, but we shall see Him. If the world will see Jesus no more how will they be attracted or drawn unto Him? Since we have face to face relationship with Him, we will see Him, but whom will the world see? The world will see us because we are being transformed into His image.

In verse 20, we have the operator, the administrator, and the One who manifests. Jesus said that the world would see you because He was going to the Father. We first have the Father. Jesus says that He is in the Father. As you look at the diagram on the next page, you will get a clear picture of this scripture. We have the Father, then Jesus and then He states that we are in Him. So we have the Father, the Son and then you. Then He says, "I am in you." In other words; the Comforter is in you; the Holy

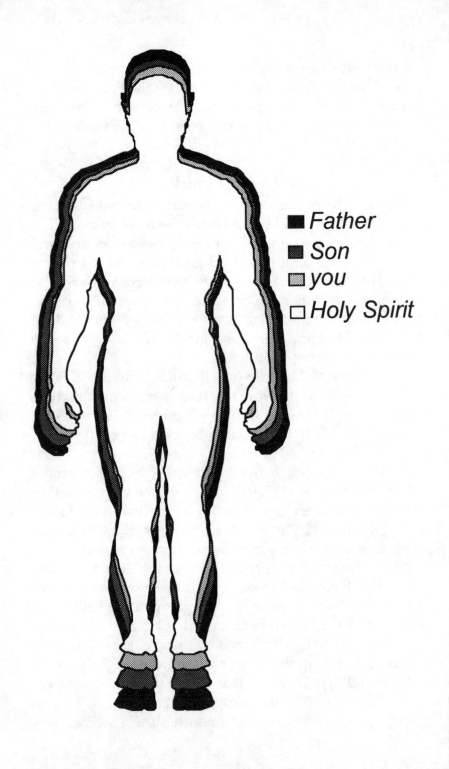

Spirit is in you. Jesus said, "I am no longer. I am removed unto my Father. I am at the right hand of the Father interceding for you." Who takes His place? That's right, you do! Jesus says, "I am in the Father; you are in Me and the Holy Spirit is in you." Now that Jesus is no longer in the earth and He is removed, we must take the place of administration on the earth. Jesus will give you the administration since you are here in His stead. Sometimes the Lord will give you the freedom to administrate the release of the gift. Other times we must follow His instructions to the tee.

Obedience

We have to obey His voice, His leading; we cannot do it on our own. We must listen to what God is saying. God doesn't ask us to throw away our own personality. If God wanted a robot, He would have created them to touch the world. Jesus had His own personality in what He did. God is not asking us all to be robots or to be inhuman. All He wants is for us to do His work with His heart and intentions. So He is the One who says, "Tracey, go and lay hands on that lady or call that man over here." Then when they come, I have to listen for further instruction, if He does not give me detailed instruction, I can step out in faith. He might just say, "I want you to lay hands on him or her." Sometimes He says "I do not want you to lay hands on them." Sometimes, He says, "You are to stomp your foot and they shall be healed," or, "Blow on him or her and they will be touched."

Many times I didn't do what the Lord had asked of me. I remember there was a time that I was at a meeting, and the minister called on a few people to help him pray for a demon-possessed man. For a while, I just stood back and watched, then the Lord spoke to me saying, "Hit him in the stomach." Some may have jumped at this opportunity, but I was a little intimidated by this command and refused to obey. I remembered Smith Wigglesworth who hit people with glorious results of healing and deliverance, but I just couldn't work past the fear in my mind. I was bold but this was just too wild for me at the time. So I compromised. I walked up to the man, balled up my fist and stuck it into his stomach. I pushed with very little force and said, "Be free." The man received some freedom by the time everyone was done praying for him, but he was not completely free. Since then the Lord has never asked me to do that again, but if He does, I will obey. So if you're in our meeting and I hit you, just know that it's the Lord!

A Mind To Help People

God wants His people to do the work. Don't be afraid to step out in faith if you don't understand everything that God desires of you. He is a loving and merciful God. Whatever it takes to touch people is what He is interested in. Let us not lose His heart and get caught up in the gifts or caught up in how uncomfortable it can be. Let us not lose God's heart in our zeal to be used of God. I am sure it would have been uncomfortable for Jesus when He spat on the ground and mixed it with dirt and put it in a blind man's eyes if He would have had a selfish agenda. The blind man that Jesus healed didn't care that He spat in dirt and made mud when his eyesight was restored. Everyone that witnessed this miracle may have said, "Oh, He spat," but the person being healed is saying, "I don't care, spit on me, and pinch me, anything as long as I get healed and set free." People get caught up on the methods more than the results, straining at gnats. This is what the Pharisees did. This is what religious spirits do, they do not see the end result. But God has called us to great things, things that our natural minds will not always understand.

Overcoming Fear Of Failure

As long as you are wrapped up in the Father and the Son, with the Holy Spirit inside of you, you can step out in faith and not bring harm to anyone as long as your heart is sincere. Do not be afraid to step out and miss it. The fear of failure is the biggest thing that will hinder. If you can get past the fear of failure, God can take you to unlimited places. You and I are afraid to be shamed, look bad, or have people exclaim that you missed it. It is not an easy thing to step out. You must fight the fear of failure. At times, we are our worst enemy. That is why it is important to know who we are in accordance with God's opinions, not man's. You are wrapped up in God and filled with His very presence. He loves you so much that He is around you and in you. He is not going to allow you to "miss it" when you are doing your very best to walk in obedience to Him. He loves you so much that He gave you authority and then He gave you power. So now that you know that you have a badge and a gun you are ready to pull the hammer back and take care of business.

Spiritual Gifts; Not Offices

In 1 Corinthians 13:8, Paul describes the different gifts to which we have access. Most of the time, spiritual gifts are given at a predetermined time in our life. Every child of God is called to operate in spiritual gifts and to preach and witness to Christ's resurrection. This is not a matter of an official calling to church leadership. These gifts are necessary to function as effective witnesses of Christ. The only requirements are to be born again, filled with the Holy Spirit and receive a measure of faith. Please don't confuse these spiritual gifts with the motivational gifts listed in Romans 12, nor with the spiritual offices that are listed in Ephesians 4:11. For Example: A person called to the office of a prophet will operate in the gift of prophecy, but people that operate in the gift of prophecy aren't necessarily called to the office of a prophet. It is not necessary to be called to one of the five offices of church government to be used of God.

When Is The Gift Given

Every Christian has been given specific spiritual gifts to minister in, but at times God has need to use us in gifts that are unfamiliar to us. Throughout the course of my walk, I have experienced the blessing of being used in most of the gifts of the Spirit. You will not always operate in all of them on a regular basis, but there are certain gifts given to each person that God has entrusted you with. I believe that the gifts of the Spirit are delivered at a point of contact with the Holy Spirit, at salvation, at the time of being filled with the Holy Ghost, by the laying on of hands, or when an individual has a special encounter with the Holy Ghost.

For instance, William Branham didn't receive his gifts of revelation and healing until the angel of the Lord appeared to him in the forest and he had been ministering for some years. Kathryn Kuhlman didn't see anyone healed in the first years of her ministry. Healings began to take place after a revelation of her dependency on the Holy Spirit. The Lord may have already imparted the gifts to you that He desires for you to operate in, but often there is a time of revelation that needs to happen for you, which will bring the gift or gifts to the surface.

Covet Earnestly

God has placed a wonderful emotion in your soul called passion or zeal. 1 Corinthians 14:1 uses the word zeloo (dzay-lo'-o) which means to have warmth of feeling for or against, covet earnestly. The Ten Commandments tells us not to covet anything that belongs to someone else, but here God speaks of another law, which gives us the freedom to covet the things of the Kingdom of God. God speaks very loudly through pure desires. It is most likely that if you have a desire to be used, it is more God's idea than yours. As long as you are seeking to know God and His Kingdom, your motives should be pure. If your motives are not right you may find yourself very frustrated, but if you are seeking God and delighting in Him then watch out! God just might shock you with what He will do with you and through you.

Psalms 37:4
"Delight yourself also in the LORD, and He shall give you the desires of your heart." **(NKJ)**

When you delight yourself in the Lord, the Lord will bless you with the things that you desire. It is easy to get tripped up on thinking that everything you desire comes from your flesh. You must realize that now that you are a child of God, the Lord creates in you the desire to want the things that He has chosen for you. Philippians 2:13 says "for it is God who works in you to will and to act according to his good purpose." (NIV) Paul says to covet earnestly, because God has put that coveting inside of you.

Prepare For All Of The Gifts

Now don't be distressed when at different times God leads you to operate in something that you have never been used in or that you have no desire for. At different times, the Holy Spirit will need a work done, and you may be the only one available. You may not normally operate in the gift of healings, but God may call on you to operate in that gift because there might be a person that will die if you don't step out.

Some of you may be wondering, "How will I know that He desires for me to step out?" The first way is very obvious. If you see a person with a tumor on their neck and you feel an incredible urge to pray for that person or if compassion fills your soul, then step out in faith. Jesus Himself was and is moved by compassion. John G. Lake said that compassion is the key to healing. The second way is through the gifts of revelation. Imagine that you are walking down the street and as you pass a young man you hear the voice of God, or see a quick vision flash before your eyes showing you that the young man is distressed and is contemplating suicide. At that time, you can continue to go on with your life or you can stop him and minister life to him.

Led By Wisdom

Wisdom is especially needed when operating in the gifts of the Spirit in the secular world. The goal is not to let everyone know that you are gifted. The object is to help people. So use wisdom as you approach people. I always try to strike up a conversation before I hit them with the Word of the Lord. At that time, I would ask the Holy Spirit to open the door. If time is short I will just walk up to them with a big smile on my face and greet them. People are often very suspicious and nervous so don't ruin your witness with arrogance. I always ask their permission to tell them the word or what I feel. I also use words like; "Can I tell you something?" or "Can I encourage you with something?" If they are not willing to hear, don't force the door open. Allow the Holy Spirit to open the door. The Spirit leads us in this way.

Led By The Spirit

The third way to know the Lord desires you to step out is by the anointing. Each one of the gifts has a particular tangible presence of the Holy Spirit that accompanies it. For example: you are standing in a line for a concert and the presence of God comes on you as you are waiting to go in. Unless there is a gift of revelation accompanying this presence, you will have to ask the persons around you whether or not they are in need. As you become aware of this anointing, it may start to move into your hands. Your hands might turn red and get hot. They may tingle a little. This type of manifestation usually accompanies one of the gifts of power, mainly the gift of healings. So look around you to see if anyone is noticeably ill in any way. If you don't notice anything, then ask the persons next to you in the line if they are feeling all right. Don't be shy about it. You never know what will happen. Cancer may be destroying someone's body and they will be healed when you pray for them. Do yourself a favor, don't make the moving of the Holy Ghost so mystical that you become afraid to step out.

Remember: it only takes faith. Right now where you are, say out loud "Jesus is Lord." Very easy to say, wouldn't you say? 1 Corinthians 12:3 says, "No one can say that Jesus is Lord except by the Holy Spirit." Saying Jesus is Lord is not so mystical is it? Neither is our operating in the Spirit. It is supernatural, but not mystical. Just as easy as it is to say "Jesus is Lord," it is the same to see the sick healed, to receive a word of knowledge, or a prophetic word. These too can only be done through the help of the Holy Spirit.

Ready In Season And Out Of Season

We should have an understanding of all of the gifts of the Spirit in order to be ready in season and out of season. The Holy Spirit should be able to use us at anytime, no matter what gift you are used to operate in. Some people are intimidated to operate in gifts other than the one that they are used to. Let's say that you are used to operating in the gift of prophecy and the Lord calls upon you to step out in the gift of healings. While walking through the supermarket a man falls to the floor clinching his chest, it appears that this man is suffering from a heart attack. Instantly the Holy Spirit speaks to you, "Go and lay hands on that man and I will raise him up." So you step out in faith and he gets instantly healed!

If there is no one with the gift of healings in the grocery store and somebody falls over from a stroke, then God is going to call upon you, not the cashier that does not know Him. You may say, "healing is not my gift, God!" Well, that day you were called on circumstantially to operate in healing. At any given time, God can call upon you to operate in any one of the gifts. You must have an understanding of them all in order to be prepared for these opportunities. Some people prophesy once and never prophesy again. When Moses passed, the Spirit of the Lord was released on the people, they prophesied once and never did again. So some of us may operate in a different gift and never operate in it again, but God has delivered unto you at least one of these gifts to operate in on a regular basis.

We are the body of Christ. I cannot be the eye if I am the toe. I have got to be exactly what God has called me to be. When we all work together in the body, then the work of God will be accomplished in us and in the earth The days are changing and you can't always wait for one of the five-fold ministers to do all of the work.

The Purpose For Revelation

The gifts of revelation are purposed to deliver the revelation and interest of God to man. It is purposed to release revelation and understanding to man from God personally and for the benefit of others. It is allowing God's intentions, desires, and ideas to be known to man.

The Word Of Wisdom

1Corinthians 12:8

"For to one is given by the Spirit the word of wisdom"
(KJV)

The word of wisdom is the supernatural revelation or insight into the divine will and purpose of God, showing how to solve any problem that may arise. So many times in our lives we operate in the word of wisdom and never realize that it is heavenly wisdom. Heavenly wisdom enables the miracle working power of God. Very often, words of wisdom do not make sense to the natural mind. I am confident that most of you operate in words of wisdom and have never been able to explain where this insight has come from. Possibly you had a good idea, but according to all natural circumstances it seemed it would never work, but something inside of you told you to go through with it anyway. When it all was said and done, the plan worked out better than you could have imagined.

Unfortunately, we often overlook these instructional impressions for familiar human reasoning and miss the miracle workings of God. I hope that after reading this chapter we will all be more cautious, more alert and aware of any possible revelation from God. Then we won't let it drop to the floor without at least praying it through. God has so many things to tell us, but our thick traditional skulls will not allow the Holy Spirit to reveal them to us.

Persecution Comes With The Call

We are either afraid of being persecuted or afraid of being wrong. With these images of misfortune on our mind, we have chosen the route of mediocrity. Allowing the devil to steal one of the greatest joys of being saved: being able to help someone else. Persecution comes with the call to be a Christian. The only way to avoid persecution is to be completely self-absorbed and worldly. So don't be afraid of persecution and miss your blessing.

John 15:20
"Remember the word that I said to you, "'A servant is not greater than his master.' If they persecuted Me, they will also persecute you. If they kept My word, they will keep yours also.'" **(NKJ)**

Some will persecute us but then there are the 'ripe' ones who are looking for the Word. The saved and unsaved are ready to hear the Word of the Lord. Let's give them the unadulterated Word of the Lord. When Jesus said that they would hear our words, He didn't mean the words of our opinion, but the words from His mouth and throne.

Self-Generating Miracle Power

The word of wisdom is probably the easiest of the three revelation gifts to work with because it is a self-generating miracle worker. The purpose of words of wisdom is to bring heavenly wisdom into earthly circumstances. To bring instruction where it is needed. As soon as the recipient of the word follows the instruction, it instantly brings about power.

Let me tell you my hiccup story. I had hiccups for 48 hours. I tried everything to get them to stop. I went to bed and woke up with them. One day as I was driving to church with Nathalie, I said, "Lord, I have to get rid of these hiccups." Then a word of wisdom came to me instructing me to hold my breath for 40 seconds. I had tried holding my breath several times before, but not at the order of the Lord. We must follow the Word completely. Encourage the people that you minister to in the same way. When I held my breath and let go, the hiccups were gone!

The difference was I tried so many times by my own wisdom to rid myself of this annoyance, but nothing happened. This time, the Word of the Lord came to instruct me on how I could be set-free. Obedience to the word of wisdom released miracle-working power.

Words For A Solution

God has instructed many of you God with the word of wisdom and you still have not obeyed what He has commanded you to do, and you wonder why you haven't received the breakthrough that you've been praying for. Listen to your Creator, He knows best.

Words of wisdom will not reveal the problem or need to you but it will reveal the solution. You will first receive the revelation of the problem through the word of knowledge or through conversation. At the receiving of that revelation, the gift of wisdom is released to do its duty. As the hearer of the word begins to put the heavenly wisdom into action, the angels in heaven begin to bring about the miracle.

The success of the word of wisdom is strictly based upon obedience to the Word. The word of wisdom must be obeyed by the receiver in order for the miracle working power to operate. When you act upon the wisdom that God has given you, God will work a supernatural manifestation for you and change the circumstances.

Power For Promotion

We should never limit the gifts of God to the five-fold ministry. Every Christian should minister in the gifts of the Spirit. A good friend of mine is a police officer. One day while having lunch with him he explained to me that he sometimes would get very strong feelings or impressions while at work. Sometimes he would know that someone was lying to him or he would have understanding or wisdom beyond his officer training. I'm sure that some of these things were from his training, but as he described a few instances that occurred I realized that he was not only operating by instinct but also in divine revelation.

By the end of our conversation, he realized that God wanted to give him revelation at work. Think about how many lives can be saved if he just happened to be in the right place at the right time. God can warn him of dangerous situations or help him capture the suspect before the call even comes to him. He would be in the right place at the right time through the help of the word of wisdom.

Can you imagine what could happen in your life if you would allow the Lord to be involved in every part of your life through the gifts of revelation? If you are an investor, investing will never be the same. If you clean carpets for a living, carpet cleaning will never be the same. One word of wisdom could change your position at work. In the business meeting you could receive the instruction to change the whole outcome of the corporation.

The Key To Natural Problems

John 21:6

"And He said to them, "'Cast the net on the right side of the boat, and you will find some.'" So they cast, and now

they were not able to draw it in because of the multitude of fish." **(NKJ)**

This took place after the death and resurrection of Jesus. As far as the disciples were concerned, Jesus went away and they didn't know what to do other than to return back to their work as fishermen or whatever occupation they had before Jesus had called them. They had been fishing all night and were unable to catch anything. Words of wisdom have to apply to natural things as well, since most of our problems are manifested in the natural realm. Although a person can have spiritual and emotional problems, these still manifest natural effects. So when you have a word of wisdom from the Lord, it will often deal with the natural difficulties that you are facing in life, maybe your marriage and relationships, your health, your business, anything that needs the touch of God.

Verse 6: Here we see the word of wisdom, God told them exactly what to do. He gave them the wisdom to bring increase in their lives. A divine revelation of how to solve their problem of lack and bring supernatural increase. At the instruction of the Lord they cast their nets on the opposite side they were fishing on. The increase was so great that they could not bring the reward of their obedience into the boat. Wow! Are you ready for this type of increase in your life? Well, get ready it shall be as long as you obey the Lord.

Luke 5:3-8
"Then He got into one of the boats, which was Simon's, and asked him to put out a little from the land. And He sat down and taught the multitudes from the boat. When He had stopped speaking, He said to Simon, "Launch out into the deep and let down your nets for a catch." But

Simon answered and said to Him, "Master, we have toiled all night and caught nothing; nevertheless at Your word I will let down the net." And when they had done this, they caught a great number of fish, and their net was breaking. So they signaled to their partners in the other boat to come and help them. And they came and filled both the boats, so that they began to sink. When Simon Peter saw it, he fell down at Jesus' knees, saying, "Depart from me, for I am a sinful man, O Lord!" (NKJ)

I have noticed that in my life, the word of wisdom comes just in time. After I have tried everything possible to bring about the breakthrough, just when I have exhausted every option, the Lord gives a bit of insight that changes my whole perspective. Many times, we react just like Peter did in this scripture with a feeling of distress and weariness. But we must not forget that when we're at the end of the tunnel the Lord is our guiding light. Just remember that when you're tired of fighting, that's when God runs to the battle.

A Reason To Live

The most exciting thing about this is not that we can receive the word of wisdom for ourselves, the excitement comes when we have a word for someone else that is in distress. To see the hope and joy that comes on their faces when you speak the word that brings about the so desired change in their life is exhilarating.

Look for these opportunities throughout your daily routine. If you see someone distressed, ask the Lord for the opportunity to minister His wisdom to him or her. You will find that in the morning you will be more eager to jump out of bed to prepare yourself in prayer and the Word because you expect to be used during the day, fulfilling the call of God to help someone that is in need.

Don't concern yourself with what to say, the Holy Spirit will give you what to say when the time is right. Often you will find yourself in the middle of a conversation uttering wisdom that you should be applying to your own life, a clarity released into your heart at that specific moment. Other times, you will receive insight for a friend or someone during prayer. At these times, it is very important to pray it through before delivering the word to them. You may need to pray for the right time to deliver the word to the person or you may not need to tell them at all. It is very possible that the Lord is showing this to you for the sake of prayer only and you must become an intercessor until the thing that God has shown you comes to pass or until the Lord releases you from the burden. People tend to say things that God didn't tell them to say. Instead of praying what God told them to pray, they are talking. Try to stay away from this, because you could offend the person if they are not ready to hear it. Also, don't be afraid to make a mistake because God will cover your ignorance, but He will not cover your stubbornness until it is repented of. This is true with all of the revelation and prophetic gifting.

What's The Motive?

If you are not sure whether to tell it or pray about it, it is best to pray about it while asking the Lord to open the door for you to share it if that is His will. If it feels good in your heart and you have a peace about it, then you go ahead and share it. If you make a mistake, pray for more understanding and look for someone else to bless. If you get persecuted for trying to help someone and you miss, as long as you have good motives give it to God, and let your accusers talk to the Lord about it. Don't argue or justify yourself. The only perfect minister so far is Jesus and we all are pressing toward the pattern of our Savior.

Be confident when you speak on the behalf of the Lord. And never change your word unless the Lord shows you that you missed it. Most of the time, your first word is right. I will cover more on this in the prophecy chapter. Don't discredit yourself before you're sure that you have missed it, people will always doubt whether or not your words are true. The worst thing to do is to make sure that you have a way out, this behavior is always motivated by fear. Fear is your enemy and your down fall.

Go To Florida

For example, I was praying for a friend of mine that was considering a career change. She owned a hair styling salon but she desired to move into a new technique of hair cosmetics. She was planning to attend a conference in Florida to learn more about these new techniques. The Lord spoke to me, saying, "Tell her to go to Florida no matter what, and I will bless her." So I told her. Well, I felt very silly telling her to go to Florida since she had already made up her mind to go.

A few weeks later, she phoned me to ask me to pray about this trip again because everything that she was planning was falling through. She couldn't get a plane ticket, the hotels were booked and financial problems had arisen. To top it off, she found out that the same conference that she was going to in Florida was also going to be in Las Vegas just a few months from then. Logic said to go to the one in Las Vegas and save money and time since she was only a four-hour drive away from Las Vegas. The funny thing with God is that He doesn't operate in the arena of logic. He will tell you to do the most illogical things and have them produce incredible fruit!

Don't Change Your Word

I agreed to pray again, even though I never believe in praying again if I am sure that God has given a clear-cut word. I went to a place where I could be alone and clearly hear the voice of God. Just as I stepped into the room and closed the door the Lord said, "Don't change your word all of the doors will open up." So I immediately went back to the phone and told what the Lord had said. Approximately four hours later she called again and said that everything had opened even to the point that finances were supernaturally brought forth for the trip. She went and met great contacts in the business and now she has closed her salon and opened a specialty clinic. She is happily in the will of God.

Come on, when we are used to speak to nations and kings in the Name of the Lord we can't be second-guessing whether it was from the Lord just because it doesn't line up with human logic or reasoning. How can we judge the angels with our own inferior wisdom? We must have the wisdom of God for ruling and reigning. If you miss it, then be honest but don't get condemned about it, just get up, dust off, and move on. People are looking for help, so don't be afraid to help.

He Knows Your Need

Matthew 17:24-27

"When they had come to Capernaum, those who received the temple tax came to Peter and said, "Does your Teacher not pay the temple tax?" He said, "Yes." And when he had come into the house, Jesus anticipated him, saying, "What do you think, Simon? From whom do the kings of the earth take customs or taxes, from their sons or from strangers?" Peter said to Him, "From strangers." Jesus said to him, "Then the sons are free." Nevertheless, lest we offend them, go to the sea, cast in a hook, and

take the fish that comes up first. And when you have opened its mouth, you will find a piece of money; take that and give it to them for Me and you." **(NKJ)**

Even though Peter was caught in a lie, God still worked with him. It is so funny how God will choose the times that you least deserve a blessing to bless you. That way, we could never take the credit for such a great break-through. Our Lord is the greatest of teachers. He will never allow an analogy to go by unused. Peter was lying on the behalf of the Lord, claiming that Jesus had paid His tribute when the truth of the matter was that the Lord had not paid tribute. Jesus, being a great man of integrity, called Peter to the side and gave him a little lesson on integrity. After He exhorted him with words, He also encouraged him in deed.

This was an incredible example of how Jesus chose to submit to the lesser law (of this world) in order to establish a higher law (of the Spirit). Showing that He had the power to cause every created thing to answer to His beckoning call. Why did the Lord choose to have a fish deliver the breakthrough money? I believe it was for the sake of Peter. A man who first of all loved fishing, how God got the fish to cooperate is not stated nor is it important. What is important is that God was working with Peter to give him the financial breakthrough as well as the spiritual increase. Supernaturally, the Holy Ghost caused this fish to have enough money in its mouth to pay the taxes for both Jesus and Peter. The Lord did not say, "Go to the bank and I will supernaturally increase your bank account overnight." He said, "Go fishing." God used what Peter knew about fishing to reveal to him His unlimited authority. Peter was a professional fisher-man and understood all that could be known about fishing. So God defied the odds and caused Peter to believe.

Remember that God gives the word of wisdom for His sake and for those who receive the word. When the breakthrough manifests, their faith is increased and the Lord gets all the glory. That is the reason for our involvement, to give the Lord all the glory.

How Do You Recognize The Gift?

The word of wisdom is like a deposit that is put inside of you which causes clarity to come to your mind. This is the way it hits me. It may hit you in different ways. But some of you might be able to relate with my description because it doesn't feel as super-spiritual or super-spooky as you might think. Clarity comes to your mind and you know exactly what is going to solve problem. You know exactly what is going to happen. It is the wisdom from heaven that you may have tried before but it didn't work because the power of the Lord wasn't behind it. It is as if a light bulb just comes on and you say, "That is the solution." God has given you the solution; you did not figure it out with your own brilliance. It is God bringing the revelation at the right time. He gives you a divine solution to your problem and you see the problem in a new light; the light of the solution.

The Word Of Knowledge

1 Corinthians 12:8
"to another the word of knowledge through the same Spirit," **(NKJ)**

The word of knowledge is the supernatural revelation of divine knowledge or insight into God's mind, will, or plan; and also the plans of others that man could not know of himself. The word of knowledge can bring a breakthrough like nothing else can. Its purpose is to cooperate and function with other gifts of the Spirit. The word of knowledge rarely operates in and of itself. The only way that it will is through intercession, and even in the intercession it will usually activate the prophetic utterance or the gift of faith.

The word of knowledge only brings revelation of a circumstance and/or its desired end, then it will activate another gift to bring about the promise or manifestation. It is never proper to just give a word of knowledge and then leave the person without a solution. I once heard of an evangelist that would call people out of the crowd and only tell them all of the symptoms and problems in their body, then he would have them sit back down. Well, I would rather not have the word of knowledge if all I could do were to tell someone that they were sick without doing anything about it. Don't forget in the excitement of receiving a word of knowledge that it is not the end of ministry to the individual; the word of knowledge will work with the gift of healing or any of the other gifts of power, revelation, or utterance.

I saw a brief commercial on the psychics and this lady was doing nothing other than telling people what was going on in their lives, but she didn't have the words of life in her mouth to help them like we do. We have the mind of Christ and we also have the power to back up what God is saying.

The Crowbar

The word of knowledge is like a crowbar. It pries open the door of people's hearts to allow the Holy Spirit to move in. It will pry someone's heart open to hear more and to receive. It is wonderful when you run into someone who's heart is closed to the Gospel and whiie you are talking with them the Lord begins to show you the secrets of their heart and the plans that He has for them. So you begin to share with them what God is showing you. Their eyes get big and they take a few steps back. Instantly, they are willing to hear more and actually find themselves asking you questions. This is called the strong man's Gospel; this is the name that John G. Lake used to describe the Gospel preached with power. Jesus used this type of ministry while He was living on the earth.

John 4:9-10
"Then the woman of Samaria said to Him, "How is it that You, being a Jew, ask a drink from me, a Samaritan woman?" For Jews have no dealings with Samaritans. Jesus answered and said to her, "If you knew the gift of God, and who it is who says to you, 'Give Me a drink,' you would have asked Him, and He would have given you living water." **(NKJ)**

Jesus asked this woman to give Him a drink of the water that she was drawing from the well. The woman replied to Jesus according to the tradition of that time. Little did she understand that Jesus had no regard for religion or tradition. Even to this very day He has no regard for these things.

Never Thirst Again

He basically said to her, "If you knew the gift of God and not your tradition you would have known whom it was standing here talking with you and you would have been filled with the power of the Holy Ghost." The word here used for gift is the word 'dorea', which the Vine's expository describes as a word that is referring to spiritual or supernatural gifting. The word of knowledge brings about knowledge. She only could have known through the word of knowledge who this was standing before her and His intention for her life. Because of her tradition she was not familiar with the word of knowledge, which resulted in her missing the living water that would refresh her soul forever more; eternal life. She would never thirst again. Jesus could see beyond the crust of tradition that was formed over her eyes and took the time to minister to her, to bring her out of her unbelief.

John 4:14-19
"but whoever drinks of the water that I shall give him will never thirst. But the water that I shall give him will become in him a fountain of water springing up into everlasting life."
The woman said to Him, "Sir, give me this water, that I may not thirst, nor come here to draw." Jesus said to her, "Go, call your husband, and come here." The woman answered and said, "I have no husband." Jesus said to her, "You have well said, 'I have no husband,'" "for you have had five husbands, and the one whom you now have is not your husband; in that you spoke truly."
The woman said to Him, "Sir, I perceive that You are a prophet." **(NKJ)**

When this woman heard of the wonderful possibility of never thirsting again, she immediately asked for it. The prophetic promise of a better tomorrow will cause a hunger to arise in even the dullest of souls. When she asked for more, the Lord started to prepare her heart to receive through the word of knowledge. He asked her to call her husband. She replied that she didn't have a husband. Then God opened the floodgates of revelation. "You have five husbands." At this point the woman's face started to turn red and she began to get a little uncomfortable. She realized that she wasn't talking to just an ordinary man, but the Son of man; a prophet of the Lord.

At this revelation, the living water began to flow in her heart and she was filled with joy and excitement. Overflowing with this living water, she went to her city and caused the people to come out and see the Lord.

The Strongman's Gospel

The word of knowledge is a wonderful tool for evangelism. Some time ago, I was in the mall and I happened to stop at an internet kiosk where they were allowing people to get on the internet on a trial basis. So I looked up our ministry web page to see how it looked on their computer. As I was pulling up our page, the lady working the kiosk came over and started talking to me. While we were talking I thought to myself that this would be a great tool to open the door to witness. So, in my heart, I asked the Lord to open the door. Then I pointed out my web page to her and explained that I was a minister. She quickly stated that she was Jewish. Well of course I asked her if she was orthodox or secular. She stated that her father was orthodox but she was not. Instantly, the Holy Spirit spoke to me and said, "She is a lesbian." Of course I was taken a little off guard with the boldness of the Holy Ghost, but sometimes that's the way He is. So I decided to pursue that road. No, I didn't jump out and bash her over the head with every scripture in the Bible against homosexuality.

That's why the Holy Spirit won't trust a lot of people with too much revelation because they don't use wisdom when He gives them some insight. Instead, they scare away the person that God is courting into the Kingdom of God. Remember that the goodness of God will win people to the Lord sometimes more effectively than fear will, since His goodness will produce longevity.

Wisdom Wins Souls

Jesus used wisdom to win souls. Proverbs says that a wise person shall win souls. So I started asking her questions about her belief system leading to the subject of homosexuality. After a few minutes of conversation, I finally got her to the point that I could share the Word of God with her. I briefly explained to her about prophetic ministries and that God showed me that she was gay and spoke to her about a few other things in her life. At this point, it was quite fun because she was hanging on every word that I said and you could see the awe all over her face. Then the Lord said that He would heal her after I shook her hand at the end of our conversation. When I told her this, she immediately stuck out her hand because she wanted to be healed. Many people reading this might ask if I made her get on her knees and repent and say the sinners' prayer. No I didn't. However, I did lead her to the Lord. The word of knowledge opened her heart up to receive the Gospel and to hear from the Word of God like never before in her lifetime. This is power evangelism, and it works.

Knowledge For Action

Discernment is crucial when receiving a word of knowledge. There are so many ways to receive a word of knowledge; through dreams, visions, and the voice of God or a knowing (intuition). Remember not to make the gifts too mysterious, they are very simple and practical. The things of God are very practical from administration to the things of the Spirit. When I say practical, I mean that they are functional for every believer. Remember what the purpose of knowledge is. Knowledge is information that empowers us to accomplish a specific task. So when you receive a word of knowledge its not just for your information. God is not into gossiping.

With knowledge comes an anointing to accomplish. I will either receive a word through the voice of God or by a vision of the Lord. Sometimes it is just a knowing. I will know something as clear as I know that my name is Tracey. It is an imparting of revelation knowledge into your intuition or spirit and can be reasoned with the mind. The danger of this gift is that you will have the opportunity to mentally process it and at times will reason it away. When you receive a word of knowledge, it will sometimes feel like you were instantly filled up.

When you tell someone about their life and they don't know you and they know that you have no way of knowing anything about them except if God told you, they will easily come to realize that God loves them enough to speak to them.

This is such a wonderful way to help people, but please understand that it would be very easy to let a gift like this get out of hand and go to your head. Just remember these three things and you will be all right.

First, you're nothing without Jesus. Secondly, you're not more important than anyone else; God can use a donkey or a rock if He wants to. Thirdly, always give God all the glory and show public humility through thanksgiving.

In Acts 9:8, we see the works of Ananias, the man that prayed for Paul when he was blind. This is an incredible example of the word of knowledge, which came through a vision. Ananias received information that he didn't know before. The Lord showed him the name of the person He wanted him to minister to, as well as the street where the man was to be found. This is a wonderful picture of how God moves and why God moves.

At this point, I am sure that Paul was distressed at losing his sight which led him to pray to the One who temporarily took his sight. Just a side note for those people who might read this and think that this is a great example for proving your point that God puts sickness on people. God may have caused him to be blind, but God also caused him to see again. The key to seeing God move on behalf of Saul was that Saul was praying. The people who get the best words spoken over them are usually people who have been talking to God or people who have others talking to God for them.

After Ananias received the word of knowledge, which got his attention, the Lord began to prophesy to Him. I don't believe that anyone can prophecy without the help of the word of knowledge or some other revelation concerning the past, present or future. Just receiving the revelation is not prophetic, because the prophetic is a gift of utterance. It is when the word that is to be uttered moves from just revelation to creation. We will cover more of this in later chapters.

Spiritual Hunger

I had a pastor say to me, "Tracey, you're not really a prophet because all you do is announce words of knowledge." It's time for us to gain an understanding of the supernatural if we really want to be effective in these last days. Every country and every nation is growing hungry for supernatural things and the church is trying to give them food that was good in the 80's and early 90's. These programs will no longer work for the children of God or for the world that is going to cross over into a new century and a new millennium. It's time to go back to the future. Back to the Bible. The supernatural is the technology of the future. Seeker sensitive meetings and "can't we all just get along" messages will not change the heart of a beat down and hurting society. It will take men and women like Ananias to move the hard-hearted, murdering gang member and the careless, AIDS infested prostitute to the altar. We must kill the Sunday-as-usual-meetings and turn them into times of refreshing and equipping. Remove the half-digested sermons and feed the people with an eternal purpose. Get out of the suburban psychedelic fantasy of a nice little church where there will never be any nose-ringed skateboarders or overgrown hippies that reek of smoke. Pastors, if this is your dream and you want an easy ministry without casting out devils and dealing with the undignified, save the world some trouble and turn in your ordination papers, because Christ the Physician is looking for the hurting.

Ananias instantly stepped out to accomplish the word that God had commissioned him to perform. When he stepped into the room that Paul was in, he approached Paul, laid his hands on him and prayed for the healing virtue of God to set Paul free. Instantly, the power of God moved on Paul and the darkness fell from his eyes.

Straight Street Encounter

We see three gifts of the Holy Spirit working in conjunction to accomplish the will of God. First, the word of knowledge, the Lord said to Ananias, "Go to Saul at Straight Street." The second was the gift of prophecy, the Lord said, " He is My chosen vessel to go to the gentiles." Thirdly, was the gift of healing; Ananias prayed for Paul's eyes and the scales fell from his eyes. In this example, all categories of the gifts are activated through the word of knowledge. First, came a gift of revelation, second, a gift of utterance and third, a gift of power.

Do not just walk up to someone and say, "Your child is in jail" and then walk away. You have to give them something from the treasures of Heaven to hold on to, some hope and life. The word of knowledge does not pry open the door and leave it open for the wind and draft to come in, but it opens the door so that they can be ministered to.

The word of knowledge often feels like I was half full and God just came and poured the rest of the water in and now I am overflowing and bubbling. I can see so many different things but God will give a word of knowledge and I realize that God sees it all very differently. Sometimes it comes as a still small voice. For example, in one case, God said concerning a lady that when she was a little girl she had experienced a supernatural encounter with Him. That was the word of knowledge. After that the revelation came. I saw her standing by her bed and the Lord showed me a great deal of details in the room, and the Lord continued to speak a word of healing and restoration to her.

At times, I will feel the power of God rushing down my leg, then I will say to the person that I am praying for, "Do you have a problem in your right leg?" I share the knowledge that God has released to me through a tangible anointing. I will feel that physically. This is a natural manifestation of the word of knowledge.

Discerning Of Spirits
1 Corinthians 12:10
"to another discerning of spirits," (NKJ)

Discerning of spirits is the supernatural ability to distinguish between spirits, good or evil spirits. It is also the ability to know the mind of man. Many times we will go to a new territory to minister in and the Holy Spirit will show us the spiritual darkness and principality that controls that territory, or what type of angels He has released to that territory to bring the breakthrough for the Kingdom of God.

Remember that all of the gifts of revelation work with your reasoning faculties or your mind. But we are to never allow them to become reasoned thought or processed imagination. The only reason they must first come through your mind is that God has made us free moral agents. If God would ever override our decision making abilities it would be practically the same as demon possession. Another reason is that we must filter every revelation that we receive through the sifter of the written Word of God. A revelation will never oppose or be contrary to the Bible. It must fit within the puzzle of the sure word of revelation.

Lastly, His Word would never be uttered if the revelation is confined our to spirit man. Many people are receiving revelation that is contrary to the Word of God and claim to have a discerning spirit. As you speak and receive revelation from the Lord the logical part of your mind should be going through all of the scriptures to confirm the revelation. If you can't think of a scripture right off hand to confirm what you are picking up, it is best to put it on the shelf until you know that it is Godly. Know the purpose for this caution is not to be controlling or legalistic, it is so that everything we do and say is done in the character, love, and Name of Jesus.

I See You

Discerning of spirits is very similar to the word of wisdom and word of knowledge in that it will come through dreams, visions, intuition, or the voice of God. This gift is very easy to become carried away with. After seeing one demon, people tend to become demon conscious. I believe that God is showing the strategic placement of angels more than demons. On the same note it is important to know Satan's plans in order to defy the plots of the Devil.

2 Corinthians 2:11
"lest Satan should take advantage of us; for we are not ignorant of his devices." **(NKJ)**

The Lord is interested in helping us keep the upper hand on the kingdom of darkness. So, He gave us this special gift to thwart his plans. Many church splits could have been prevented if the pastors or the staff members would have operated in this gift. Remember that the enemy will use people and cause them to do things that are ungodly and unscriptural. Most of these people aren't demon possessed or even meaning to harm. They most likely think that they are doing God a favor. But God can show us how the enemy would want to use these well-meaning people.

A Total Change

We have ministered to people who have problems in their lives that have been hindering them and their family members for years. The Lord will give us insight into the source of these problems. For instance, I was praying for a young girl at a youth rally, and the Lord showed me that her family was under a curse of witchcraft that stemmed from a prior generation. It manifested itself through the form of fear and anxiety. I saw her mother and an older woman standing next to her and sensed that the curse came through her mother's family. I said to her, "Your mother is under the influence of witchcraft because of someone in her background. That spirit of witchcraft has been coming against your family and has caused oppression and depression in the following generations as well." Later, her mother came to the meeting and confirmed even the setting and place that I saw in the vision. The Lord gave discernment into the cause and gave the power to break the curse.

This family had been suffering from these problems, but didn't have an understanding into the cause. They never realized that a family member who lived in the hills practiced occult things long ago, and would have an effect on their lives generations later. But God did, and He was kind enough to deliver and reveal the spirit behind it so that they could be free. The girl approached me at another meeting and told me that she and her family have totally changed, including her mother. Their whole lives were changed because we took hold of that dirty lying spirit when God gave the discernment and broke the power of that thing.

I remember an instance when I first got saved, we were praying outside in front of my friend's house. We had a group of people show up for the prayer meeting and we were not ashamed of the Gospel, but unknown to me, one of my friends was afraid that his parents would be looking out the window and see us praying on their front lawn. I heard the voice of God saying to me, "In his heart he is afraid of his parents looking out and they would be ashamed of him." God allowed me to know what was in his heart so that I could encourage him to stay focused on the Lord. In the New Testament we see Jesus do this many times. Jesus said that He perceived what was in their hearts. Not only did He know what was in their hearts; He knew who was with Him and who was not. He knew these things by the gift of discerning of spirits.

The Holy Spirit is willing to use anyone who makes themselves available and that have a desire to use this gift for God's glory and not for personal gain. This gift will enable you to see what spirits are operating and controlling people, and enable us to discern the motivation behind their actions.

Luke 6:6-8

"Now it happened on another Sabbath, also, that He entered the synagogue and taught. And a man was there whose right hand was withered. So the scribes and Pharisees watched Him closely, whether He would heal on the Sabbath, that they might find an accusation against Him. But He knew their thoughts, and said to the man who had the withered hand, "Arise and stand here." And he arose and stood." (NKJ)

Jesus discerned that the Pharisees were trying to find fault in Him. Instead of giving into their pressure, He used the revelation to make them even more mad in order to destroy the control that they were trying to bind Him under. This gift is awesome for breaking controlling spirits or the influence of controlling people.

Known By The fruit

This gift is often in action when someone walks into the room and you suddenly have a good or bad feeling or impression of them. I believe that the fruit of the spirit will cooperate with the discerning of spirits. Peace, love and joy are just a few that will keep you in check. Even though you might feel uncomfortable with someone or something in your emotions, these fruits will help clarify whether it is your flesh or your spirit. Your flesh might cause you to not love someone that you feel uncomfortable about, almost as if it is a personal thing. With spiritual discernment you should be able to continue to love them.

You will spot someone with his or her own agenda. It is best not to say anything when you are first learning to use this gift, just take it to prayer. We tend to put more trust in our ability to confront than God's ability to change someone through prayer. Pray and watch and look for the outcome. It won't take long for their agenda to surface if your are praying. Never ever try to control someone's will through prayer because you think that you have discerned something. Just ask God to change their motives if they are impure.

Ministers, the Lord has placed someone in your life that has a discerning spirit to protect you from trouble. It could your spouse or a staff member. You would be doing yourself and your ministry a grave injustice if you take them for granted and not take what they're saying serious enough to pray about. And if you're the person that God has trusted with this gift, seek God to know about good things and not only the negative. It is much easier for humans to pick up the negative before the positive. The last thing you want is to become judgmental. Don't just go around judging everyone because of every little perky feeling you get. When you get a feeling, just spend extra time praying; let God confirm it several times before you approach the person involved.

This negative tendency is why we have so many "demon watchers" in the body of Christ. There are many more angels than demons; it's a shame that we are always looking for the devil and not God. But God is opening the eyes of the believers to see angels in these last days, to encourage us that there are more of us than there are of them.

Many intercessors operate in the gift of discernment of spirits and they get off track calling themselves a prophetic voice or a prophet or a prophetess. God has given them discernment into what is happening in the atmosphere or in a church and instead of praying, they organize a meeting with the pastor to tell him how to run the church and what changes he needs to make to get back into the will of God. If you are not anointed to speak the prophetic word, it will be powerless and end up causing more trouble than helping. If you're anointed to pray, the power of God will only move when you pray and the changes will only come through prayer.

Acts 16:16-18
"Now it happened, as we went to prayer, that a certain slave girl possessed with a spirit of divination met us, who brought her masters much profit by fortune-telling. This girl followed Paul and us, and cried out, saying, "These men are the servants of the Most High God, who proclaim to us the way of salvation." And this she did for many days. But Paul, greatly annoyed, turned and said to the spirit, "I command you in the name of Jesus Christ to come out of her." And he came out that very hour." (NKJ)

Mocking Spirits

This girl was actually telling the truth and announcing a great confirmation to the people. If we look at this just by face value, it would look as if there was nothing wrong with what she was doing. When in all actuality she was bound by a mocking spirit, which was causing unnecessary attention to Paul and the others. Paul sensed that this flattery from this girl was wrong and the gift of discerning of spirits kicked in and he knew that this false praise. Being grieved by the demon controlling this girl, Paul moved into the gift of faith and commanded the evil spirit to leave her. Once again, we see another gift coming into operation to assist in the work, first revelation, then power.

We need this gift in the church. Many people come with flattering and encouraging words, but their heart is evil. If you are naturally minded and can't discern what spirit these people are under, it could be very dangerous. It might sound nice, but the word will have some type of seduction about it that will cause the Christ-likeness in you to feel uncomfortable.

Acts 14:8-10
"And in Lystra a certain man without strength in his feet was sitting, a cripple from his mother's womb, who had never walked. This man heard Paul speaking. Paul, observing him intently and seeing that he had faith to be healed,
said with a loud voice, "Stand up straight on your feet!" And he leaped and walked." (NKJ)

How could Paul know that this man had the faith to be healed? Though the discerning of spirits. Paul could see the man's faith. There is no knowledge of what Paul was preaching but it was enough for this man to believe. The reason that most churches don't have supernatural occurrences is because they don't build the people's faith to expect the supernatural. This man's faith was so strong that the Holy Ghost was excited about it. God then anointed Paul to see and the faith anointed him with healing virtue to meet the man's faith.

False Prophets

This gift also helps us discern when something is birthed of God and when someone is under the unction of the Holy Ghost. Too often we say that it is not God when God is moving. We are living in the days that Jesus spoke of when there would be false teachers and false prophets. All we really need to follow after are the true teachers and prophets, because as long as we find the truth, we don't have to be concerned with the false. Like many of you when you watch those psychic commercials, what happens when you see those commercials? You are grieved. Are any of you compelled to call? No? That is because the Spirit of God is inside of you and He gives discernment of what is right and what is wrong. But when you are in need and a man of God tells you to call an eight hundred number for prayer, you will not hesitate to call. You are discerning the difference between the two. Do not make it too difficult. You are discerning what is God and what is not. It does run deeper than those examples, but if you can't discern in the small, you sure will miss the more complicated matters. God is raising up a generation of Christians who will operate in all the gifts of God. They are going to walk passed a psychic, discern the spirit, then cast him out and see them delivered.

We are moving closer to being a walking force ordered by the voice of God. We are going to stop that lie of the enemy that is counterfeiting the move of God. He is a counterfeiter, he has no authority and he has nothing of his own. He stole everything that he has from us. It is a shame that Christians are afraid to operate in the gifts of the Spirit, the gifts of clairvoyance. They are afraid to operate in it because they think it is psychic. We have the Author and Finisher of our faith, He is the one that has begun it, He is the one that is going to finish it, and we are the church that is going to do it.

The Jesus Anointing

People are living in fear and defeat and now they are making infomercials about it. People are afraid of all sorts of things; this is not God's will. Fear and depression is not supposed to control a human body and it's emotions. I heard a shocking statistic on the news that said that by the year 2020, chronic depression would be the number one disabling disease. I believe the reason for this is because the Church hasn't done its job; giving true spiritual hope. Much of what we've handed out is hype.

This generation is not going to allow this to happen any longer. We are going to speak the Word of the Lord and cast out devils just as our Jesus did. We will cause this statistic be turned around by the discerning the spirits and then break of this bondage of depression and fear.

The Church needs this just as much as the world does. Church after church we go to, we come across wonderful people that are bound by these oppressions. What happened to being anointed like Jesus, going about doing good and healing all those that are oppressed of the devil? We teach that Jesus did it, but the Church itself has forsaken it for the hope of a bigger house and better life. If we would equip the saints the way the Bible says, then we would have prosperity and increase. I have never seen in the Bible the blueprint for a church that is seeker sensitive. You never will; the church in Acts was prosperous because they had revival. Nehemiah told the people to stop bringing more supplies because there was too much, which was caused by revival. There are churches that have people driving to the service in nice cars, but they live like the devil the rest of the week. I am hoping that all Christians that desire a better life will have it but not at the expense of the truth.

We are supposed to give to God everything. And when we do that, we will see His victory in our lives. The world is trying in every way to deceive people. If they are going to put that on television how much more can we put something that is real on the television? How much more can we stand up and say we know the living God, Who operates in the real gifts? He is the Author of the gifts. Open your heart and present yourself as an available vessel. God wants us to have a heart of availability. Present yourself as available not able. Only by God's strength are we able.

Revelation Gifts: Practical Application

Recognition: Recognize these gifts by the desires of your heart. The Lord allows us to have a desire for the things of God, then He leads us and teaches us how to fulfill these desires. Some gifts will be easier to operate in because of your natural inclination or personality, and your motivational and/or five-fold gifting. The understanding in this is to go after what come easy to you. If it's easy to prophecy and you desire to pray for the sick, step into the prophetic and study healing. Soon they both will be operating strongly in your life. Lastly, you can recognize your gifts by what urge you have when the anointing comes upon you. What happens when you feel the anointing, for the revelation gifts, you may experience clarity in mind, a feeling of knowing something very strongly, visions may flash in front of you. You may even tend to daydream and find yourself watching an open vision, as if it was a movie as you see into the spirit world.

Operation: Be willing to approach anyone when the Lord leads, be willing to pray when the Lord leads, and be willing to hold your peace until the Lord leads you to speak. Remember that most of the time the gifts of revelation will not operate alone, they will activate or cause a reaction in you, the recipient, or the power of God to bring about the miracle. In stepping out in faith, always be gracious and loving.

Development: There are three things that we can do to activate these revelation gifts. Ask God to use you and to give you revelation, believe that He will use you, and step out in faith as you recognize His leading. The best way to train your ear and intuition to the gifts of revelation is in intercession. When we approach God on the behalf of someone else, God sees a selfless heart and begins to show us what to pray for through the use of these gifts. I believe that within a thirty-minute time span of intercession any person will operate in at least one, if not all, of the gifts of revelation. If you can't minister to people in prayer for half an hour, how can the Lord use you on the street where there are distractions all around?

Learn in private then allow God to interrupt you in public. The best way to develop these gifts is by communion with the Holy Spirit. Just spend time listening to Him. If at first you don't notice a difference, continue listening. The Holy Sprit wants to know that you want to know Him and not just receive His gifts. So spend time building trust and in due time, you will find yourself conversing with the third Person of the Godhead. Once you hear His voice in this way you will be able to hear His voice in ministering.

Another good way of training yourself is to pray while someone that operates in these gifts is ministering. I would watch the "This is Your Day" program and as soon as Benny Hinn starting praying for the sick with the words of knowledge, I asked the Holy Spirit to give me the same words. At first I was completely wrong, but after some time I started getting more and more accurate. One day I was watching television and the Lord spoke to me and told me to go to the bowling alley. After a time of arguing, I decided to go. I believe the Lord knew that I would argue for at least thirty minutes, so he told me thirty minutes a head of time. When I got to the bowling alley the Lord showed me who to talk to. I was very nervous so I just walked around and played video games, hoping that this fellow would just leave. This guy was on a date and the Lord wanted me to tell him something. I just imagined how I would feel if some one gave me a word from God out of the blue. That is a little weird; that's why the Lord doesn't ask for our opinions, He just wants us to obey.

I saw them preparing to leave so I went outside and waited for them. When he came out, I hit him with the Word of the Lord, and he was wonderfully ministered to. But before I could give him the word, I needed to get off my couch.

Don't ever stop training your gift, I watch William Branham's videos all the time because I want more. Lastly, spend time listening instead of always talking and pull out your Bible and study meditate on the word of God. As you are trustworthy with little, God will trust you with more!

"None of the gifts of God
should operate
without hearing
the instruction of the
Holy Spirit."

Chapter Five

THE GIFTS OF POWER

1 Corinthians 12:9-10 *"to another faith by the same Spirit, to another gifts of healings by the same Spirit, to another the working of miracles,"* **(NKJ)**

The Holy Spirit revealed to me that this power only comes from praying and reading the Bible for hours each day. Make spending time with God a priority without time limits. I began to seek the Lord for extended times a day. I studied the book of Acts and noticed that every other book had an ending, but this one. Which is a good way of saying, "This is just the beginning." I looked in the Church for the manifestations of God that I read about in the book of Acts, but I couldn't find many. This was very interesting to me because we claim to believe the Bible, but I didn't see the action that should come from faith. The Bible says that we should walk in the same power that Jesus ministered in, but many modern day churches say that we should not. So which one is wrong?

John 14:12
"Most assuredly, I say to you, he who believes in Me, the works that I do he will do also; and greater works than these he will do, because I go to My Father." **(NKJ)**

Many believe that this means that the church as a *whole* would do greater works, not necessarily individuals. That theory doesn't make sense, because since my conversion I have seen the works of Jesus, as well as the greater works. We have seen many people healed and set free. We have seen people set free from the oppressions of the devil. We have also seen the greater works. For those of you wondering how far God will take us in using us as instruments of His glory, I am persuaded that we can walk with the Holy Spirit without measure if we do whatever it takes.

In Your Footsteps, Lord

Right from the start I had made up my mind to see the same things that the Apostles experienced. I would start each day by praying for the Lord use me as He used the Apostles; "I will go on the streets, use me to touch others, minister through me, do whatever You want with me, I am Yours!" Then the Lord led me to start riding the bus to a nearby city to witness on the street; it would take me an hour and a half to get there. The Lord would start moving before I reached the downtown area. I would read my Bible all the way. I would ask Lord to send me someone that I could talk to. Someone would sit right next to me and they would ask how I was doing, and that was my open door.

On the bus I saw people saved and I started praying for the sick. I started laying my hands on them. I would always introduce myself as Christian, thinking that it would give me instant credibility. Little did I know that it would turn most of them off. It did not discourage me, I was looking for the one individual who was open and ready. I remember praying for this elderly lady on the bus wearing a hearing aid. I approach her to ask if I could pray for her. She replied, yes, and confessed to be a Christian also. So I put my fingers in her ears. I could see everyone around us getting very uncomfortable. This didn't bother me, I was too focused on seeing the power of God. I said, "In the Name of Jesus, I command these ears to hear!" I did the same thing that I saw Benny Hinn do. This was all I knew to do. I was just a few months old in the Lord. That didn't discourage me because Paul started preaching almost immediately after he was saved. When I was done praying the lady thanked me, then put her hearing aids back in her ears and went her way. I went back home very upset by this undeniable shame and disappointment. However, I had faith, an unmovable faith. I said "God, You are either God or a liar!" (This is not my advice to you, in my ignorance I spoke very foolishly to Almighty God, but He looked at my heart, what love!).

First Disappointments

You see, I had thrown Christianity out of my life at an early age. By the age of thirteen I confessed to be an atheist. I was devastated by the death of my first best friend: my grandfather. As he was on his sickbed and dying, I remember for many years falling on my knees between the ages of 7 to 11, asking God to heal him from cancer. I was calling on God to do something that the traditional church at the time didn't teach. But I believed that if God could create, He could also fix things. My grandfather eventually died, but not before he was wonderfully saved. But salvation wasn't what I wanted at that time. I wanted to be able to call on the name of my best friend. This was a major blow against my faith. With this disappointment in my heart I left my grandmother's, who used to take me to church, to live with my mother, who was a Muslim. The God of the Bible disappointed me and the god of the Koran never answered me, so I threw

God out of my life altogether. Of course the Lord later changed my mind and is using that experience as a motivation to kick the devil's tail as often as possible!

Zeal Without Knowledge

When I got back to my house and went into my room to confront the Creator of the universe, I was speaking as a young man that had been looking for the Truth all of his life. And I wasn't about to commit to a lying God. So I said, "You are either the God of promise, the same that moved in the Book of Acts and all through Your Word: the healing God, or a lying God. I will not serve You if You're a liar. I will go out and serve the devil." I had already been serving him through sinful living. I had looked into self-preservation, self-help, and new age thinking.

The devil had already tried to recruit me and promised to give me power. I knew the devil would give me power and when he was tired of using me, he would try to kill me. I truly didn't want to go that route so I said God, "If You are the true God, if You are the One the Bible says that You are, You will start using me, and I will serve You all my life." We have to have that type of fight in us, that type of determination. Not that you talk to God that way, no, He is not our son. We are His children, submitted to Him. I was just fresh from the streets. I did not have enough sense to know I should have a fear (reverence) of God. But God liked my boldness; He saw my stupidity and said, "I could use this guy." God wanted His Truth shared and all I wanted was the Truth, this was truly a match made in heaven. Do you want the truth enough to keep on pressing on until you see the God of Elijah? This generation has the heart of Elisha; we are looking for the God that moved the Red Sea. We are looking for the God of Elijah.

No One Got Healed

After going through all this, I would go back out to preach and pray for the sick. My goal was to see someone raised out of a wheelchair before my sixth month anniversary of being born again. That was what drove me. I separated myself to pray, read, and seek God. My grandmother would call me for dinner or the phone, but I asked her not to disturb me while I was praying to God. Then I would go to the city again looking for someone to minister to. I prayed for many people and they still didn't get healed. Then I would go through the same process again of going back to my room and crying out to God again. Saying, "I will not give up until You move. I will not quit until I know that You are true or false. I am not going to stop until You heal them and if You do not I am walking!"

I have been a Muslim, an atheist, and then some. I wanted to know if He was true. I was relentless. I did not see any results, some people have immediate results, but I did not. I kept going because I fell in love with the presence of the Lord. I already loved Him. I remembered how I felt when I got saved. It was like liquid love running through me cleansing me from my guilt and shame. I said, "If this is a lie like all the others, I do not know what I am going to do." So I held on. You have got to hold on and keep on pressing on.

Power And Peanut Butter

Finally, one day, as I was in the kitchen at a friend's house making a peanut butter sandwich, another one of our friends came over. She walked into the kitchen and said she had a headache. Jokingly, I lifted my hand and put it to her forehead and said, "In the Name of Jesus be healed." She fell to the floor under the power of God. When she got up, she said she felt as if she had a hole in her head and the headache was completely gone. I was rejoicing. Finally there was power!

I believe that God was seeing how hungry I was, and I sure was hungry by this time. We immediately invited all of our friends over to have a prayer meeting on the lawn. We saw people's legs grow out and other miracles that we had believed for. All of the miracles I had been waiting for and pressing into God for, started happening as people went under the power of God. I was faithful in little, which caused God to bring the increase. The Lord truly wants us to touch people more than we desire.

A Loving Pastor

There were many signs and wonders, people falling under the power of God, being delivered. The first real miracle was undocumented, a young boy that was deaf from birth. After praying for him, he could hear things that he couldn't hear before. I was very excited because this was similar to the first miracle that I had seen on Benny Hinn's television show. But the miracles and dramatic healings were sporadic. I wanted to see people's lives changed. From there on things got worse for me because I left the streets and started ministering in my church. I had just started going to a new church and was very aggressive and zealous. My pastor would preach a great sermon and then call the people to respond to an altar call. When the people started forward to the altars, the anointing fell on me and my hands started tingling. So instead of finding someone in the crowd sitting next to me to minister to, I assumed that the Lord wanted me to take over the alter call by praying for the people. The Pastor did not know me. It was probably my second time in this church. (Please don't do this in your church) I ran to the front and started from one end and laid hands on about fifty people, they all fell out under the power of God. The pastor was such a lovely person; he let me do it the first time only because the Lord told him not to stop me. Fortunately for me, he was very sensitive to the Holy Spirit to obey the voice of God.

The next week I did the same thing. This pastor still didn't feel released from God to stop me. Many other pastors would have stopped what God was trying to develop in me. Obeying God was more important than his reputation. The third time he said, "Tracey that is enough." Later he called me to his office and told me why he didn't stop me at first. He said that he wanted to invest in me and to teach me about what I was operating in. He started sharing with me what was orderly and what was out of order. So he put me in classes to learn more about leading people to the Lord and seeing them filled with the Holy Spirit and put me on the altar worker's prayer team. He didn't squish my gifts; he gave me room to develop. My pastor never stopped me, but the older Christians in the church started arguing and questioning my motives.

You will make mistakes and some people might not get healed but the fact is, that most of the Christians in the body of Christ are unwilling to take a risk. That will be the brunt of your persecution coming from people who most likely mean well. So don't throw the spear back at Saul. Keep a sharp edge on your gift by continuing your ministry wherever you are and pray for the Church. Lord willing, you will have a pastor like I did.

If you are a pastor reading this book, I will encourage you with a little wisdom from my personal experience. The people that you sincerely invest in and who you seek to develop beyond your vision, will in turn help your vision and be forever loyal to you. People can tell whether you care about them or just want to use them. It's wonderful to find someone that is willing to work and get involved. A moving car can be steered; a parked car is impossible to steer. Steer rather than stop.

Purpose Of Power

The gifts of power are for the purpose of releasing God's power to man on the behalf of God, resulting in spiritual and natural breakthroughs, for the sole purpose of defusing and destroying the works of the devil.

The Gift Of Faith

1 Corinthians 12:9
"to another faith by the same Spirit," **(NKJ)**

The gift of faith is the supernatural ability to believe God without human doubt, unbelief, or reasoning. The gift of faith is an extension to the measure of faith that has been delivered to every believer. When this gift kicks in, you have faith to believe for unimaginable things. The gift of faith has the ability to supersede natural and supernatural laws. It will give you the unmovable faith to move whatever mountain God is leading you confront, as well as give you the confidence to draw from the spirit-realm into the natural.

We need this type of faith to believe God for nations to be opened to the Gospel. This faith caused the walls of communism in Russia to fall and will cause the iron curtain of China to open. This is the gift that causes people to fall over in the power of the Holy Spirit. We called it 'slain in the Spirit'. The Holy Spirit takes control over our natural body, causing it to submit to the will of the Holy Spirit, allowing God to operate as He wills.

Hebrews 11:3
"By faith we understand that the worlds were framed by

the word of God, so that the things which are seen were not made of things which are visible." (NKJ)

This gift of faith will cause us to speak the things that are not as if they are, causing them to manifest through God's power. The gift of faith cannot be worked up; it is delivered to us by the Holy Spirit for the purpose of God.

Matthew 21:19-20
"And seeing a fig tree by the road, He came to it and found nothing on it but leaves, and said to it, "'Let no fruit grow on you ever again.'" And immediately the fig tree withered away. And when the disciples saw it, they marveled, saying, "'How did the fig tree wither away so soon?'"(NKJ)

Absolute Faith

This gift of assurance doesn't give any room for doubt whatsoever. Jesus spoke to the fig tree, commanding it to obey His absolute faith. Absolute faith will not allow nature, demons or fear to resist it. We speak in the Name of Jesus and everything around it submits. I have prayed for sick people under the gift of faith when they didn't have the faith to believe God themselves for their healing. As I prayed, a doubtless confidence hit my soul and they were healed. It was as if they borrowed the faith that the Lord delivered to me for their healing. I want to make it clear that I didn't pray against their will, they were willing, they just didn't have faith to believe they could receive.

The gift of faith is powerful but it cannot override the will of a human being. God Himself would never override the moral obligation of man. In the same way, His gifts will not. As the tree withered, it caused the disciples to marvel. The gift of faith is a marvelous gift. It truly shows God as the God of the impossible. The other thing that we can see in this scripture is that they marveled at the speedy obedience of the withered tree.

The gift of faith moved this tree. In verse 21, Jesus assured the disciples that if they had faith as a mustard seed, then they could move a mountain. All we need is a portion of this faith that comes as a gift from God. We have a mustard seed of faith without the gift. The mustard seed is one of the smallest seeds there is. You and I can move a mountain with that amount of faith. We all have that much faith. Now when the gift of faith hits us, how many mountains can we move? I know at some time the gift of faith has come upon you. There is a time when you experience a faith where you say, "I do not care what the circumstances are; I am about to get a breakthrough." You will become very angry at the obstacle.

Righteous Anger

One day, a lady came to me with a fibroid tumor the size of a large orange. She informed me that she was scheduled for surgery the following Tuesday. I laid my hands on her forehead to pray for her. I wasn't persuaded that she would be healed. I prayed a prayer of faith in the Name of Jesus, hoping that the women would have the faith to pull on God. As I looked into her face, I saw the tears streaming down her face and her lips were grasping for any help from the Lord. I prayed, "Father, in the Name of Jesus, I ask that You would heal this woman and set her free." Then something hit me; a supernatural incredible faith came out of nowhere. God put this supernatural faith in me that this woman would walk out completely healed.

When the gift of faith hits all asking stops and the commanding starts. The gift of faith commands with the same creative power as the Father commanded the earth and the universe. So I said, "In the Name of Jesus, GO!" She went down to the floor under the power of God. She was unaware of the effect of the prayer. She went to the doctor the following Tuesday. She requested for the doctor to check her before they went in to remove the tumor. They optically searched for the growth and found only some scar tissue, which they remove that day. Thank you Jesus for your power to change lives! The life of God caused the life in the tumor to wither away, God had completely healed her and showed His love to her. That was the gift of faith that suddenly hit me. I did not have the faith at first, but God desired to heal her so He gave me the faith necessary to bring about the miracle.

Unsaved And Healed

Years ago, I had the opportunity to minister several times to a substance abuse support group, which met at the church that I attended. In this group was a man who suffered with heart problems. The Lord released a word of knowledge in one of the meetings revealing this man's problem. The gift of faith hit me after the word came; I hit him in the chest and said, "In the Name of Jesus be healed." A few weeks later he came to the meeting and told me that his heart was completely healed. Three weeks after that he came to me again and told me that he got saved that day. He got saved after he was healed. Most unsaved people are willing to take a chance on being healed and will get healed easier than Christians do. The gift of faith will cause you to do things before you have a chance to even reason them away. There is no chance for you to doubt or be afraid.

Prayer Of Faith Or Gift Of Faith

Acts 3:4-7

"And fixing his eyes on him, with John, Peter said,

"'Look at us.'" So he gave them his attention, expecting to receive something from them. Then Peter said, "'Silver and gold I do not have, but what I do have I give you: In the name of Jesus Christ of Nazareth, rise up and walk.'" And he took him by the right hand and lifted him up, and immediately his feet and anklebones received strength. (NKJ)

The gift of faith hit Peter so fast that he did not have a chance to decide whether or not he should step out. Instantly, the lame man was healed. The Holy Spirit supernaturally distributes this gift, but the prayer of faith is a prayer that any believer can pray at any given time. There is a great difference between the two. James 5 says that if there are any sick among you ...the prayer of faith shall make them whole. It is not based upon anointing, but a mustard seed faith. You do not pray for it, you command it. You do not pray a prayer, through the gift of faith, you release it.

Smith Wigglesworth operated strongly in the gift of faith. If we ever had the chance to sit under his ministry, you would have seen people healed by a fist blow to whatever part of the body that was ailing them. So if you suffered with a stomachache, he punched you in the stomach. Of course this wasn't the only way that he ministered, but this did occur while he was operating under the gift of faith.

Under the gift of faith people do wild things. This is very true in this story of Peter ministering to this lame man. With complete boldness he pulled the man to his feet. The man rose immediately, according to the faith that was delivered to Peter.

Strange Methods

Another such account is when Jesus healed a blind man

in a shocking manner. We hear very often of some pastor or leader getting upset at a method of an evangelist or a supernatural minister. Usually the reason is because many people try to reason the moving of the Holy Spirit, trying to cause Him to operate within the limitations of human logic. This is why for so many years the church has turned its back to the prophetic and apostolic ministries.

Both the prophetic and apostolic ministry operate strongly within the realms of the spirit, establishing true spiritual government. Not governmental authority based upon what your friends say, it is based upon what God says to you and based upon how the devil reacts when you confront him. Many ministers don't understand spiritual authority so when it comes to discerning what's going on in a meeting or in their territory, they are as passive as a mannequin in the department store window. When they rise up against the devil, he checks his list and laughs, even worse, many ministers are so deceived that they think that if they have large ministries it means that they have regional or territorial authority. The devil laughs as he hears their little wimpy prayers for God's movement. The gift of faith gives us power. Look at Jesus.

Mark 8:22-25
"Then He came to Bethsaida; and they brought a blind man to Him, and begged Him to touch him. So He took the blind man by the hand and led him out of the town. And when He had spit on his eyes and put His hands on him, He asked him if he saw anything. And he looked up and said, "'I see men like trees, walking.'" Then He put His hands on his eyes again and made him look up. And he was restored and saw everyone clearly. (NKJ)

"A Rushing Mighty Wind"

Look at how bizarre this miracle came to pass. When the gift of faith is in operation you can practically sneeze toward someone that is sick and they will be healed. Many times I will stomp my foot by the leading of the Holy Spirit and the people will be touched. When I first started praying for people, they would go down under the power of God, then stiff necked religious people started to say that I was pushing people over. Well this was silly to me because first of all I knew that God didn't need me to push people over, second of all people can get healed just as wonderfully standing up. Seeing that I hate religion, I asked the Lord to anoint me to blow on people so that I could stand some distance away from the people and He could be seen touching them. Weeks went by and I had forgotten about this prayer.

As I was praying for a group of people, a burning started in my chest and increased until I began to breath a little heavy. Then I heard the Holy Spirit say, "A rushing mighty wind and no one can stand in the Presence of an awesome God." I didn't understand what He said at first, but I soon understood that He was releasing me to breathe on people. So I did and people began to get healed that way. People started falling under the power of God by one breath. This stopped the religious accusations for a short while. We forget that Jesus is not religious and He wants to destroy all false beliefs. This was the gift of faith in operation, since then people have received breakthroughs through shaking hands, running, counting, clapping and even snapping fingers. Remember when it was considered uncivilized to snap your fingers? Now God uses it to touch people. I think I'll start handing gum out in church services so that God can touch His people. In numerous of odd ways God has moved and I think He likes it that way. There are many uses for the gift of faith. The gift of faith casts out demons, heals the sick, brings divine confidence for anything that a person can believe for, causing it to come into being according to the will of God, even to the point of raising the dead.

Acts 20:7-12
"Now on the first day of the week, when the disciples came together to break bread, Paul, ready to depart the next day, spoke to them and continued his message until midnight. There were many lamps in the upper room where they were gathered together. And in a window sat a certain young man named Eutychus, who was sinking into a deep sleep. He was overcome by sleep; and as Paul continued speaking, he fell down from the third story and was taken up dead. But Paul went down, fell on him, and embracing him said, 'Do not trouble yourselves, for his life is in him.' Now when he had come up, had broken bread and eaten, and talked a long while, even till daybreak, he departed. And they brought the young man in alive, and they were not a little comforted. (NKJ)

Gift Of Confidence

This is a great example of a young man brought back to life by the gift of faith. He had fallen out of a window and was found dead. When Paul approached the young man's dead body, Paul could see by faith something contrary to what everyone else was seeing. Of course he also saw that the young man was dead in front of him, but the gift of faith, that is the supernatural ability to believe for the impossible, caused him to see beyond the circumstances into future. With this confidence he spoke out the words, "Do not trouble yourselves, for his life is in him." The boy didn't immediately rise to his feet and go on with life. Paul spoke these words and left the lifeless body where it laid and went to have something to eat. It even says that Paul had broken bread and talked for a long time. Who knows when this young man came in but it was obvious that is was quite sometime after Paul had left. Could you imagine the reaction of the people, Paul fell on him, embraced him, spoke a few words and then left. I'm sure many of the believers around were wondering what this fellow was doing. Had Paul given up? But Paul was so confident that he just walked off, knowing that the work had been done and that it had to manifest sooner or later. To bring true understanding to the gift of faith is to translate it as the gift of confidence, and we can see that Paul did not lack confidence in this story at all. Such supernatural confidence that superceded any doubt that may have been in the crowd.

When the anointing for faith comes, you will have a supernatural confidence that whatever you ask in prayer, as long as you believe, will be delivered to you or to whomever you believe it for. This anointing may manifest tangibly, but for the most part it is a conviction in the soul that demands response.

The Gifts Of Healings

1 Corinthians 12:9
"to another gifts of healings by the same Spirit," **(NKJ)**

Faith To Heal

The gifts of healings are a supernatural power to heal all manner of sickness without human aid or medicine. This gift comes through the anointing. One example is Benny Hinn, he operates in the gifts of healings. In his crusades, there is an atmosphere or presence for healing. My wife,

Nathalie, normally operates in the gifts of healings and has seen many healed under her hands. As we reflected on the miracles and healings, while writing this book, she described an exciting miracle that had taken place a few years back. She was praying for a lady that had been through several surgeries that left her with a severely damaged knee. Certain parts in her knee had been removed to the point that it was impossible for her to bend or kneel on her right knee. There was continual pain so that she could not sleep at night without taking strong pain pills. As Nathalie laid her hands on the lady's knee, boldness for a miracle came upon her. Under Nathalie's hands, the sound of cracking bone was heard and her knee was instantly restored. She quickly tested it by having the lady bend and rest on the healed knee. The wonderful Miracle Worker put in brand new bone and cartilage! The woman was so overjoyed that she asked if she could accept Jesus as her Lord and Savior as well. The power of God is the witness to bring people to Jesus.

There is an anointing available for strictly healing the sick. The gifts of healings work differently than the other gifts of power, in that it has one sole purpose: to heal all manner of sickness. Healing can manifest instantly as a miracle, or it can take a period of time. The gifts of healings are not isolated to physical illnesses. The gifts of healings cure any aliments: bodily, emotionally, and mentally. It is described as the gifts of healings for this purpose. The Holy Spirit, depending on what He can trust you with distributes the different gifts of healings.

Mark 3:14-15
"Then He appointed twelve, that they might be with Him and that He might send them out to preach, and to have power to heal illnesses and to cast out demons:" **(NKJ)**

This clearly states that the Lord gave power to the disciples to heal illnesses, it doesn't say some sickness. It would be unscriptural for us to assume that God would distribute to his followers something less than what He, Himself, would operate in if he expects us to accomplish greater things than He accomplished here on the earth.

Mark 16:17-18
"And these signs will follow those who believe: In My name they will cast out demons; they will speak with new tongues; they will take up serpents; and if they drink anything deadly, it will by no means hurt them; they will lay hands on the sick, and they will recover." **(NKJ)**

Anointed For A Reason

The Lord will use any believer to heal the sick. Through God's promises, we as believers have authority to cure the sick, but there also comes a gift that will help each individual fulfill their individual destiny. All are called to pray for the sick, but few are chosen to have this gift as their primary calling. This means that every Christian should pray for the sick, but not everyone is to make it his or her entire ministry in life. The anointing only comes for ministry. This is also true for the anointing that activates the gifts of healings. This unction comes from the initiation of the Holy Spirit, not only by our reasoning of the truth that is found in the Word of God. People with this ministry will always be aware of sick persons around them. They are always looking for the opportunity to destroy this oppression of the devil.

Luke 5:16-20
"So He Himself often withdrew into the wilderness and prayed. Now it happened on a certain day, as He was

teaching, that there were Pharisees and teachers of the law sitting by, who had come out of every town of Galilee, Judea, and Jerusalem. And the power of the Lord was present to heal them. Then behold, men brought on a bed a man who was paralyzed, whom they sought to bring in and lay before Him. And when they could not find how they might bring him in, because of the crowd, they went up on the housetop and let him down with his bed through the tiling into the midst before Jesus. When He saw their faith, He said to him, "'Man, your sins are forgiven you.'"(NKJ)

What's The Secret?

There are several very important points in this passage of scripture that will give us an understanding of why the power of the Lord was present and why the man was healed. The first point we find in v.16, Jesus separated Himself to pray. This was a key factor in the life and ministry of Jesus. Between His times of prayer, He walked through life working miracles. You must be prepared to pray if you want the power.

Secondly, in v.17, we see that Jesus was teaching. One thing that I have learned is that you must teach on the blessing that you want the people to receive. If you desire for God to use you in healing, then teach on healing. If you want God to work miracles, then teach on miracles. If you want people to get saved then teach on salvation. The same goes with financial increase. What you teach is what you get! I have seen this in action with many ministers including in our own ministry. This principle is not confined to the five-fold ministry. One-on-one ministry is one of the most effective forms of touching a person's life. It is simple to teach on the benefits of salvation.

Create Expectation

Prayer and teaching on salvation activated the power of the Lord being present to heal. Please understand that I am not describing a formula. These are principals and lifestyles that bring a reward when practically applied. The key is that whatever you sow, you reap. At this point, we notice the sick looking for Jesus. Once you start teaching about healing whether you have been used in this type of ministry before or not, people will start coming to you with the expectation to receive their healing. The greatest things that I have noticed in meetings conducted by men of God like Reinhard Bonnke, Benny Hinn, and T.L. Osborn, is that there is a great expectation built up to receive. The faith bank is high. In v.20, Jesus saw the faith of the man to receive his healing. Believe me, it is much easier to work with faith than it is to work with doubt.

Thirdly, work with the faith of the receiver. They must understand that their faith is important in receiving their healing, just as your faith is instrumental in helping them receive. For this reason, your teaching will be very important, especially for the Christian. Based on my experience I believe that non-believers are easy to get healed because most of them don't have any religious doctrines to overcome that tell them they can't receive. Which brings us to the next point; Jesus healed this man by forgiving his sins. If we can cause the Christian community to understand that with the receiving of Jesus comes salvation for spirit, soul and body, then we can destroy guilt, shame, unbelief, religion, and tradition, which are major obstacles to receiving healing.

Isaiah 53:4-5
"Surely He has borne our griefs and carried our sorrows; yet we esteemed Him stricken, smitten by God, and

afflicted. But He was wounded for our transgressions, he was bruised for our iniquities; the chastisement for our peace was upon Him, and by His stripes we are healed." (NKJ)

Freedom In Your Body

These verses are very important to the believer. This version says that He has borne our griefs. The Hebrew word for griefs is **'choliy'** (khol-ee'), which means malady, anxiety, calamity. Jesus has taken these things from us. This is the true life insurance policy from Heaven. Every physical sickness is covered with this policy. The wonderful thing is that there is not even a deductible, it has already been paid!

Freedom In Your Soul

Then it says that Jesus has carried our sorrows, has taken on the burden, and has completely removed the yoke of sorrows off of our backs. The word sorrow in the Hebrew is **'mak'ob'** (mak-obe'), which means anguish. This is dealing with the realms of our soul. Again, this is covered under the same policy without a deductible. This covers any affliction that deals with the mind, will, and emotions. Our soul can receive a free overhaul of the power of God. This dose includes Alzheimer's, insanity, mental anxiety, schizophrenia, depression, oppression, possession, paranoia, and any other lie of the devil.

Vs. 5 says, "He was wounded for our transgressions", the word transgression here means **'pesha`'** (peh'-shah), a revolt, rebellion, sin, transgression, trespass. The word iniquity is **`avon'** (aw-vone'); perversity, i.e. (moral) evil. This scripture is dealing with the spirit of man and gives us a solution to be free from the spiritual ills that we have sown and what the devil has trapped us and our forefathers in. It promises us eternal salvation, the right to walk with Jesus in eternity. This salvation awakens the dead spirit of man and joins it to the life of the Holy Spirit forever more. This takes care of past, present or future sins against God's nature and will. Now that we are joined to the Master we need the policy to keep us connected. This is all free from the hand of the Father of grace. Jesus has paid the price for salvation of spirit, soul and body.

This is what gave Jesus the confidence to say, "Your sins are forgiven you," because He knew that everything for spirit, soul and body was covered in that promise. When we minister to unbelievers we need to let them know that God will heal them because He wants them to be saved from every wicked work of the devil. Let them know that their sins and evils are forgiven as they receive Him.

John 20:22-23
"And when He had said this, He breathed on them, and said to them, "'Receive the Holy Spirit. If you forgive the sins of any, they are forgiven them; if you retain the sins of any, they are retained.'" (NKJ)

Jesus released the Holy Spirit into the disciples; this was the day of salvation for them, when the Holy Spirit joined with their spirit man. When this happens to us, the Holy Spirit empowers us with authority, or delegated influence. This allows us to release God's forgiveness of sin, just as we have been studying in Jesus' life or we can retain sin as Paul did in Acts 13:11; commanding Elymas the sorcerer to go blind after he attempted to hinder the furtherance of the Gospel. Both of these acts can only be done under the leading and instruction of the Holy Spirit. This authority is not to be taken lightly nor is it for the sake of manipulation. Many think that these days are over, I must warn you that the coming of the true apostolic and prophetic ministry is at hand and are the last offices yet to be put in place, and we will see more of this authority. Paul looked at Elymas and addressed him as the son of the devil and an enemy to righteousness. Forgiving sin is for all that will receive, but retained sins are for the evil in heart, the impenitent hearts. All we have to do is keep looking for people to help and bring them to the knowledge of God.

Faith That Heals

The power of the Lord must be present for the healing to happen. When the Holy Spirit is around He always brings gifts for His children. This time we see that he brought the power to heal or the gifts of healings. The gifts of healings bring faith to heal all manners of illnesses. I believe that God increases the faith and the anointing based upon a person's faithfulness. This is true with any part of the faith walk. This gift will give faith for healing but not faith for other things. How much do the gifts of healings have to do with someone wanting to receive their healing? I believe that it has everything to do with it. If a person doesn't want to be healed, then it is virtually impossible. Now if a person wants to be healed and doesn't have faith then, as I said before, I believe that God can override this lack of faith and do what I call a mercy healing. The unsaved receive mercy healings from the gifts of healings.

There are times where the gift is hindered by unbelief, bitterness, unwillingness to forgive and many other reasons. Even though they have a desire to be completely healed there are many reasons why the Holy Spirit wouldn't be able to heal them; this is one of the reason we need the gifts of revelation to work with the other gifts.

After you have prayed for an individual and you know that the gift was active and they are not instantly healed, it is best to first build their faith, by teaching or sharing testimonies of others that have been healed. Assure them that God desires to heal them. Send them home with scriptures to study. Many people feel very unworthy to receive and we all are unworthy, but Jesus makes us worthy. Have them test the problem area several times since they might not realize that God is at work in their body. Always ask them to do what they couldn't do before. When you have them do this, include that they shouldn't look for the symptoms, they should look for the healing. Finally, for the next 24-48 hours have them thank the Lord for healing them. We have had many people healed by just taking a little extra time with instruction. We have sent people home sick with the instruction of just thanking God and the next day they returned to the meeting completely healed.

Thanksgiving is a great faith builder. God releases His power when their faith rises and the healing virtue is released to them. I prayed for a little girl who had a lump on her shoulder. When she left the lump was still there, but I told her to continue thanking Jesus for her healing. I saw her later and asked how long it took for the lump to disappear, she said it took three days, but she kept thanking God until it finally went away. That is faith as a mustard seed.

The enemy will always come to try to steal your healing just like he lies about your salvation, speaking in tongues and every blessing from above, but continue to thank God and write down when the healing took place (the moment you prayed).

Matthew 12:13
"Then He said to the man, "'Stretch out your hand.'" And he stretched it out, and it was restored as whole as the other. **(NKJ)**

Your Sins Are Forgiven You

A man with a withered hand came to Jesus with complete faith. When Jesus prayed for him, the man's hand was made whole through the gifts of healings. God released the virtue of healing into the man and his hand was released and restored. Some of the incidents are similar, but different in their display and have the same results.

For example: the man came and Jesus said: "Thy sins are forgiven. Often the reason why people are encumbered or overcome with sickness or lack of health is because of sins. The gifts of healings are like that, they are gifts that release healing to forgive and cover sin. His blood cleansed us and operates through the gifts of healings. Does that mean you can tell someone their sins are forgiven and they will go to heaven? No, I am saying if someone is bound by guilt and their sickness has its roots in sin but God wants to minister to them and heal them, you can say, "Your sins are forgiven, be healed."

God gave me a revelation about something in a lady's past. She had anger against her father and God said the reason the germs were released and began to generate inside her body and take control of her, was because of anger. God gave revelation and when I told her, she was cleansed in her heart and healed in her body. The gifts of healings is the power to cure all type of natural aliments, to forgive sins and cause restoration in the physical, emotional and spiritual realm.

Matthew 17:18
"And Jesus rebuked the demon, and it came out of him; and the child was cured from that very hour." (NKJ)

Demons are cast out by one word through the gifts of healings, so is anything that is trying to take control of a person's spirit, soul or body. It is broken off by the gifts of healings. Jesus ordered the demon to leave the boy and immediately the boy was cured.

Demons abiding in the flesh of a person, cause sickness. Cancer is an evil spirit; many families suffer with this spirit for generations. The fact that Jesus overcame sickness is the reason why we can cast them out of our bodies, by use of the gifts and authority of God. All sickness comes from demonic activities and sin. Through the Word and the gift of healings, the church will be free from sickness and demonic oppression and walk in divine health.

In The Living Classics Quotes from John G. Lake, by Harrison House, we read that healing was the evidence of God's forgiveness- heaven's testimony that their sins were remembered no more.

Heaven has sent forth a testimony that our sins have been forgiven, this testimony is healing, even the gifts of healings. Know that when the Lord calls you to operate in faith to heal all manner of sickness, that He has called you to forgive the sins or the cause of sin in their body, soul, or spirit. This gift may also manifest with tangible feelings, such as heat or tingling on the palm of the hands, or as a confidence in the soul that the person or persons you pray for, will positively be healed without a shadow of a doubt.

Working Of Miracles; The End Result

1 Corinthians 12:10
"to another the working of miracles," **(NKJ)**

This is the supernatural power to intervene in the ordinary course of nature and to counteract natural laws if necessary. Any manifestation of power is a sign and wonder. Jesus said that there would be false teachers that would bring about false signs and wonders. Since the signs and wonders that we do in the body of Christ are led by the Holy Spirit, to give glory to Jesus Christ, according to the intentions of our God, they are not false or misleading. Both the gift of faith and the gift of healings can bring about a miracle.

In <u>The Living Classics Quotes from John G. Lake</u>; John G. Lake classified difference between a miracles and healing in this way; "Healing is the restoration of what has already been and a miracle is the creative power that brings about what has never been or is missing." Miracles supersede the natural causing the natural to submit to the supernatural, allowing an effect (end result) to come about. There is no reasonable explanation for miracles. The Bible calls them infallible proofs; proof that cannot be refuted.

Acts 1:3
"to whom He also presented Himself alive after His suffering by many infallible proofs, being seen by them during forty days and speaking of the things pertaining to the kingdom of God." **(NKJ)**

Well Able Warriors

These infallible proofs (signs and wonders) are to show that Jesus is our resurrected King and that He is the Lord of all. No one can refute a miracle wrought by God. The devil, doctors, nor the religious can deny the powerful arm of the Lord. The religious couldn't answer what was done through Peter and John for the man at the gate Beautiful. Nor will they be able to reason the great acts that God will work through this last day generation. We are well and able warriors who are equipped with the miracle working power of God. A Lazarus raising generation. The raising of the dead is a work of miraculous power that will become a daily happening in the coming move of God.

None of the gifts of God should operate without hearing the instruction of the Holy Spirit. In studying the workings of miracles I learned that it is completely dependent on us hearing Him, unlike the gifts of faith or healings, in which the Holy Spirit allows us to facilitate the application at certain times. In this next passage the Lord released the miracle working power to Peter.

Matthew 14:28-29
"And Peter answered Him and said, "'Lord, if it is You, command me to come to You on the water.'" So He said, "'Come.'" And when Peter had come down out of the boat, he walked on the water to go to Jesus." **(NKJ)**

Walking On Water

When the Lord commanded Peter to step out of the boat, the miracle working power was immediately available to hold Peter above the water. The moment that Peter stepped out is when he received the end result of this miracle working power. Miracle power comes when you have heard the voice of God and follow His instruction. We will deal with this in more detail in the following chapter on the gift of prophecy. Peter walked on the water because he believed the word that Jesus spoke,

"Come." As soon as he heard the word, faith rose up in his heart. Because of this faith God's miracle power caused him to walk above the laws of nature and enter into the supernatural realms of Jesus.

John 2:5-9
"His mother said to the servants, '"Whatever He says to you, do it."' Now there were set there six waterpots of stone, according to the manner of purification of the Jews, containing twenty or thirty gallons apiece. Jesus said to them, '"Fill the waterpots with water."' And they filled them up to the brim. And He said to them, '"Draw some out now, and take it to the master of the feast."' And they took it. When the master of the feast had tasted the water that was made wine, and did not know where it came from (but the servants who had drawn the water knew), the master of the feast called the bridegroom." **(NKJ)**

Water Into Wine

Again we see that the miracle was wrought after simple obedience to the Word of the Lord. This is a supernatural occurrence; water has no way of becoming wine. Jesus worked an awesome miracle through the power of God. Workings of miracles actually mean the effect of dunamis power. The word effect is very important because it doesn't put an emphasis on the means to the miracle, it only concentrates on the end result of the dunamis power of God: the miracle.

The self-generating power of God (dunamis) causes miracles. The other operations are from an endowment (ability), where God enables us to facilitate His plan through dunamis power; an effect is the end result of dunamis power. God is going to decide how He desires to facilitate the miracle and we must obey Him.

The other operations of power are classified as gifts, where miracles come from workings; working out the action in complete obedience to Christ. Gift means gratuity or spiritual endowment, it is given to us to operate. They have been delivered to us for the purpose of using them as we are led by the Spirit. Workings are the end result of fulfilling a command. The other gifts can bring about the same effect of the working of miracles as we facilitate them.

Adventures Of Obedience

Philip was commanded to Gaza by the angel of the Lord. So he prepared himself and went on this journey. The incredible thing about this part of the story is that Philip didn't even know why he was going, he just obeyed.

Acts 8:26-27
"Now an angel of the Lord spoke to Philip, saying, "'Arise and go toward the south along the road which goes down from Jerusalem to Gaza.'" This is desert. So he arose and went." (NKJ)

He didn't gripe or complain unlike many of us. He understood that if he could learn to trust the voice of the Lord that miracles would follow. When he reached Jerusalem he ran into his assignment. Whenever the Lord tells you to go somewhere and He doesn't tell you why, then know for sure that you're like an angel on assignment. We rarely hear of these things today, simply because we don't obey like the first church. We will have these types of encounters as we learn to obey the governing voice of God. After Philip completed his assignment, a great working of miracles took place. The effect was to get him back home as soon as possible because God had another assignment for him.

Acts 8:38-40
"So he commanded the chariot to stand still. And both Philip and the eunuch went down into the water, and he baptized him. Now when they came up out of the water, the Spirit of the Lord caught Philip away, so that the eunuch saw him no more; and he went on his way rejoicing. But Philip was found at Azotus. And passing through, he preached in all the cities till he came to Caesarea." (NKJ)

My Translation:
Philip was obedient to the voice of God to go to Gaza and when he was finished with his work, the Lord changed the structure of his body and translated him to Azotus. At Azotus there were people ordained to hear him preach the Word of the Lord. I do believe that the Lord can at any given time cause us to be used in the workings of miracles. If you study John G. Lake's life, you would notice that many times he would find himself translated to another town and ministering to someone the Lord has ordained for him to touch. His lifestyle was one of submission and obedience. If you don't mind God interrupting your life with surprises and you are willing to flow with Him in these bizarre circumstances, then I believe that you can look forward to some very exciting adventures in the near future. The days of workings of miracles are here and increasing every day.

Practical Application

Recognition: Recognize these gifts by the desires of your heart. The Lord allows us to have a desire for the things of God and then He leads us and teaches us how to fulfill these desires. Some gifts will be easier to operate in because of your personality, motivational and/or five-fold gifting. These power gifts will usually have a tangible expression accompanying them, such as tingling or heat in the hands and palms. This same heat could manifest in the same location in your body that is hurting in the person needing prayer. The working of miracles is much different in that it usually will give the persons involved in an outward reward. Again the working of miracles will bring faith to supercede the natural laws bringing supernatural benefits. The key to these operations is prayer and obedience. Obey the Lord and His command will bring about miracles.

Operation: Power gifts are activated by stepping out in faith. Pray for everyone that you can and you will find God's anointing when you expect it and when you don't expect it. After a while, the Holy Spirit will lead you with His unction. Be obedient to everything that God tells you to do and the workings of miracles will become a part of your daily life.

Development: The Holy Spirit is the best teacher, as you step out in faith to touch people, He will be there to teach and lead you. In your prayer times, ask the Holy Spirit to teach you in private about the different forms of anointing and gifts. In private I learned to minister to hurting people before I even had an opportunity to minister to them in person. If you can't be foolish with just you and the Lord, you will never be able to overcome the fear of failure and insecurity that sometimes accompanies ministering in public.

In my private prayer times I saw many people pulled out of wheel chairs. By the instruction of the Holy Spirit I commanded demons to leave people's lives, one time I was even used to bring a dead person back to life! The best way to learn anything is by role-playing; the same goes for the gifts of the Holy Spirit. Practice and role-play in private so that when the time arises that God needs you to go to work, you will know what to do.

"God wants to use you,
not a religious
version of you."

Chapter Six

THE GIFTS OF UTTERANCE

Shortly after I was saved, I was at a Phil Driscoll concert. Sitting amongst a crowd of 2500 people, the prophetic anointing came upon me. I stood up and started speaking loudly in tongues as Phil Driscoll was talking between songs. I had never had an interpretation of tongues before. Every time I was used to give message in tongues, someone else would give the interpretation, nor had I ever released a prophetic word. So this was a real step in faith to speak out in tongues in front of 2500 people. After I gave the message in tongues, I quickly sat down and waited for someone to interpret. All I knew was that I felt the power of God all over me to speak. I didn't understand the difference between a corporate prophetic word and a tongue and interpretation. The effect is the same but the administration of them is different. So there I was with hundreds of people looking my way, waiting for the interpretation.

Just as I started to become nervous Phil Driscoll gave the interpretation and followed the word of the Lord with an altar call. It was a powerful moment of obedience for me. The Lord is not interested in our dignity. He was testing me to see if I would obey Him no matter what the circumstances. Do not be ashamed to look stupid when you know that God is moving you, He will always cover your back as long as you are stepping out by His unction. Even if you make a mistake God will cover your shame. He is a loving God.

The first time God asked me to stand up and speak in tongues like that I didn't realize what was happening to me. I was in a service of the pastor who has been so gracious to work with me in my first years as a Christian, he helped me develop my character and trained me in the proper use of the spiritual gifts. My heart started pounding. I didn't know if I was under fear or some ungodly control; it was a very intense and tangible feeling. I began praying for God to take this feeling from me. Immediately, it left. At that moment, I realized that it was not from the devil, but that it was God moving on me, but for what reason? So I asked the Holy Spirit what that was and He started to give me insight that this was the gift of tongues and He wanted me to speak out in tongues. The Holy Spirit has always been my teacher and, believe me, He is the best of all teachers. So I vowed that if He would give me another chance, I would obey. My greatest fear was to disappoint God so I would do anything that He asked of me. I was more afraid of missing God then I was displeasing man.

The following week I was so nervous and scared again, my heart started pounding, I got sweaty and it felt like I was having an anxiety attack while my pastor preached away. I wanted to get this over with so I stood up and I started yelling in tongues. During this brief moment of ecstasy, I felt as if my spirit man was pulled out of my body and thrown back in three or four times. I had worked myself into such a state of emotion that I was totally drained!

My hope in sharing these embarrassing stories with you is that you will first of all, lose all fear of making a mistake and secondly, to show you some pitfalls to avoid. Please don't follow my example of ignorance, but follow the example of never giving up. When all of the yelling was done I sat back down. I didn't notice the reaction of the pastor nor anyone else because my eyes were closed and I had no intention of looking around. There was the longest silence that I had ever experienced. Finally, someone stood and uttered the message. I was so relieved! Later my pastor pulled me to the side and said, "I like it that you are stepping out in this way, but there is a proper time to release the word. When I am speaking is not the time. Wait until there is a gap in the service." I encourage you the same way: wait until there is an opening that will not disturb the flow of the Spirit or the order of meeting.

The gift of prophecy, diverse kinds of tongues and interpretation of tongues are recognized as the gifts of utterance. Their purpose is to declare, proclaim, and establish God's will and intentions through verbal communication. It is God speaking and instructing man by use of another human being. These gifts do not only operate for revelation's sake; their sole purpose is to declare the given revelation with power.

Prophecy

This is a supernatural utterance in the native tongue; it is a miracle of divine utterance, not conceived by human reason or thought. It includes speaking unto men for edification, exhortation, comfort and future events.

The exciting thing about the gift of prophecy is that it works with so many other gifts. Because of this uniqueness, it creates faith that results in a miracle. If you study the prophetic ministry of the Old and New Testament, you see that each time the Word of the Lord was spoken, it created an atmosphere for God to move.

The result was either a miracle or judgment. The words of God create and it changes people, atmosphere, mindsets and life in general. That is, if the receiver believes that God has spoken. The gift of prophecy works miracles. The gift of prophecy works within a tightly knit network of spiritual gifts. First of all, everything that you prophesy must first be revealed to your spirit and soul.

So the first thing that will happen is that you will receive a revelation through one of the revelation gifts. Now you may say, "What if the person told me that they were in trouble before I gave them the word that God was going to bring them out next week?" Unless you are just making up something nice to encourage them, God had to reveal the fact that He was going to work something out before it happens. Now the fact that you have knowledge of the problem and outcome is not prophetic. Prophetic is when you speak it and it comes to pass. Many operate in words of knowledge and revelation gifts. The key is, did God anoint you to speak it? If He did, then there will follow one of the power gifts, most likely the working of miracles. Unless God says that He will heal and gives instruction to lay hands, which of course would be the gift of healing, then the gift of faith is released to pray the release of the promise upon the person. Whatever the power gift is that follows, there should always be a release of power to bring about the promise. If God is not telling you to speak the promise, please do not speak, you'll only cause more harm then help. Focus on prayer instead.

Remember that there is an anointing that accompanies each one of these gifts. The Holy Spirit will teach you about the different gifts and enable you to recognize which anointing goes with which gift. The only access to the gifts of the Holy Spirit is through His anointing. Jesus Himself was anointed. The only question is, how do you know that you are anointed? You should always be able to recognize when the anointing is upon you for work. Some people will say, "I am always anointed." Yes, this is true, in that, you are set apart for the work. You are a chosen vessel waiting for the Master's use, but only at the will of the Holy Spirit are you truly anointed. Please understand that I know that we are filled and anointed, the problem is that we cannot just go around doing what we want with God's anointing and gifts. Be led by the Spirit or you will find yourself in the flesh!

When the anointing comes to prophesy the Lord will speak to you with a word or a vision. In the beginning, you may only receive one word or simple impression. Be faithful with these 'baby visions' and God will increase them. For example, You see a stream, it is down the road, then it is coming into the person's house flowing all over their family. Although this may not make any sense to you, don't hesitate to share these dark sayings. The person receiving will understand completely what God is trying to get across. These prophetic visions or words are called dark sayings or proverbs: word pictures that give a message. It may be dark or not understandable to anyone except the hearer. You are following a picture, for some it would be like a movie and as you see you describe the vision. These forms of the prophetic can be very encouraging to you, as well as the hearer when released in the heart and intent of God. A prophecy that is anointed by God, brings a certain emotion or zeal that will correspond with the word. The deliverer of the prophetic word should feel the heart of God during the delivery. If not, it is just as false as if you didn't have the facts right.

It is also possible that you will hear the voice of God. Sometimes, it can be one word that He gives you, and when you start to deliver the word, God will give you the rest. I have experienced this many times. For example, I will hear the word, "increase", and when I approach the person to deliver the word, the Lord gives me the rest of the word.

Seek for the increase in the words that God gives you. Trust the Lord for more detailed revelation. The more specific the words are, the more it will help the receiver to believe that it was for them. Not that I am saying that simple words are not effective, because any word from the Lord is effective. There's just nothing like the feeling you get when the Lord has pinpointed your life and declares a great promise over you.

1 Corinthians 14:7-10
"And even things without life giving sound, whether pipe or harp, except they give a distinction in the sounds, how shall it be known what is piped or harped?
For if the trumpet give an uncertain sound, who shall prepare himself to the battle? So likewise ye, except ye utter by the tongue words easy to be understood, how shall it be known what is spoken? for ye shall speak into the air. There are, it may be, so many kinds of voices in the world, and none of them is without signification."
(KJV)

The encouragement comes when we give a distinct sound that could be understood. This is reason enough to seek the Lord for more distinctions in our sound.

The gifts of revelation work with the gift of prophecy. As soon as they are given for the purpose of speech, it becomes a gift of utterance. The misunderstanding is that prophetic revelation isn't given before it is delivered. But as I covered in earlier chapters, it would be spiritually illegal for God to take control of your conscience and will. Your mind must receive the revelation before you utter it. The key is to receive the revelation and speak it without trying to subject it to your human logic and reasoning.

The prophetic gift is increased by the reason of use. If you want the gift to increase, use the gift! After a while, you may be given people's names and addresses to confirm the Word of the Lord. Which brings us to the next point, in the beginning of operating in the gift of prophecy, you might not have a confirmation to follow your gift. But as you become comfortable with your gift, you should ask the Lord for some type of confirmation to build the faith of the people. Moses had a confirmation. Samuel confirmed what would take place in Saul's life before he was crowned king.

Acts 15:32
"And Judas and Silas, being prophets also themselves, exhorted the brethren with many words, and confirmed them." **(KJV)**

In this passage the word 'confirmed' means to reestablish. God used something to reestablish the words that He had already spoken. It could be distinct words like addresses and names, or it could be the gift of healing or faith. There is no limitation; God wants to make Himself plain and clear.

Always speak as you would normally speak. God wants to use you, not a religious version of you. Speak in your native tongue, King James English is not your native tongue. If you speak Ebonics (so called street lingo), then you should prophesy accordingly. For example, "Yeah bro', ya know what I'm sayin', 'cause God's down in the hood and He's about to take this place out..." Speak the way you are accustomed. Go back to the original text of the Bible or be normal. Say what God is saying as clear as you can, but stay away from adding things to it in the flesh. No matter how many times you trip over your words, if you receive the miracle working power behind it, you will see the evidence.

The other thing is that you don't necessarily need to add, "Thus says God." People will know if you're speaking in the Name of the Lord or not. Many people put so much emphasis on saying this, that it can be a distraction. If you are afraid to even call it a Word of the Lord because it is new or you may be not sure, don't be pressured to label it as such. Just say, "I feel." Just be free, and allow God to use you. But by no means be reckless with the Word of the Lord, just be free.

The gift of prophecy includes speaking unto men to edification, exhortation and comfort. That is very important. The prophetic ministry of the New Testament is different in many ways from the Old Testament prophetic ministry. I believe that most Christians will never be called upon by the Lord to rebuke someone prophetically. If judgement is to come through the prophetic, it should come through the prophetic office, not the gift of prophecy used by someone that is not called to the five-fold ministry. God is always interested in His goodness drawing someone to repentance before He chooses to release His judgement. If God must judge, it will be His last resort. The eyes of the New Testament prophetic voices must be filtered by the grace of God.
Yes, sometimes you will see that God will judge, but it is done in the character and nature of God; love and grace! Judgement doesn't come before God has tried to edify them, encourage them and exhort them out of their lifestyle of sin and disobedience. We see God's judgement in action in the story of Ananias and Sapphira. That was real judgement in the body of Christ. It is going to come back to the church, Do not be afraid, just make sure

you live holy and righteous. It is New Testament! The majority of the ministry that you are given in the prophetic word will follow under the categories of edification, exhortation and comfort.

Exhortation is instruction, edification is lifting someone up and comforting is consoling someone. If they need love and care, then you give it to them. Whatever is going to edify them to a better place. If God ever gives you a word of warning for someone, He never puts him or her in a place of condemnation. He always gives them a way out.

Let me give you an example of a godly rebuke that gives a way out. "Ma'am you have been living in adultery. God says get out or you will find yourself in a terrible physical condition because I see the enemy coming, and he is going to try to destroy your body. You must give up this relationship and come out of adultery. If you get out of adultery, God will take you to another level where you no longer will have the guilt, the shame, it all will be removed, and God's plan will be established for your life." There is never condemnation. There is only edification. All you are doing is warning them of the repercussions of their actions. But, when you hear from God, there will be a way out. The Holy Spirit never condemns, He always convicts and gives people a way out of their state of reproach. When you minister the Word of the Lord, comfort them. Sometimes people just need to know that Jesus loves them. Sometimes people just need to know that God wants to wrap His arms around them.

Example: A lady the other day. I kept looking at her, I knew she did not want to receive from God. Finally, I asked her if she would allow me to pray for her. She refused the prayer, but I still gave the prophetic word, which was that Jesus loved her and wanted to wrap His arms around her. Never hold back the prophetic word unless God tells you to hold it until a better time. God actually reprimanded me for not giving a word to someone, because His words are life giving and can change someone's life whether they want to come up front to receive or not. You can still speak it out and if they want to receive it, it is up to them.

If you have a word do not be ashamed just to say it. The word will take care of itself, you may never know how your obedience has helped until you get to heaven.

Is everybody that prophesies a prophet? NO. Does every prophet prophesy? Yes. Even if they prophesy through their conversation, there is always a prophetic utterance coming out of them. But, if you have the gift of prophecy, it does not actually make you a prophet or prophetess. So do not get confused. Stepping out of the calling of God into your own desires is very dangerous for you and anyone who could be misled by you.

If you feel that God has given you a word for your pastor or any other minister in the five-fold ministry, approach this very cautiously. Not because you could not have a word for them, but so many people claim to have words for them and it is often nothing but a distraction to the minister. The best way to handle something like this is to write it down for them. If you approach them, expecting them to listen to your word, you just might be disappointed unless you have a good rapport with them. Half of the job of giving a prophetic word is to remove anything that would cause the receiver not to trust the word of the Lord because of the 'package' that the word comes in. Always seek to build trust. Don't charge in thinking that you're God's man or woman who's going to save the day. It doesn't help at all! The humble route is always the best route.

If this is dealing with your pastor, writing down the word works great if they don't know you as a prophetic person. Usually, it is not as urgent as we think, and there will be plenty of time for them to pray about it. After a while of doing this, you will see how they respond to your gift. This is called building rapport. After a few times, they will look forward to hearing from you.

Many churches go through trouble because of intercessors with prophetic gifts who step out the will of God, thinking that they are anointed to rebuke the pastor or minister. Sorry, but if this is you, you're out of order. So step back into rank. Unfortunately, the people that do this have a problem with authority. Often times, their own life is messed up.

Never assume the responsibility of the office of the prophetic ministry to a local church, unless the minister in charge has recognized you as the prophetic minister of the church. Remember, if God is revealing something to you about the church it is most likely for prayer purposes. Not to confront, nor to gossip, just for prayer.

If the pastor begins to recognize your prophetic gift, and receives the word from you, handle this responsibility with care. This doesn't mean that you are now the counsel to the pastor. It does not mean that you can go and counsel him on his marriage, or on how to run the church. That is not your position. I am very serious about the proper use of the prophetic gift, because it is so easily misused and has caused great damage to the Body of Christ. There are many prophets, and the prophetic gifts have been pushed out the church because of misuse. This has been unfair for the true prophetic ministers who desire help and build the Kingdom of God. I want us to be able to understand where our boundaries are and how we should operate with the gift of God's voice.

Why would God desire to use you to prophesy to someone? Prophecy gives direction when there is none, prophecy gives hope when hope is gone, prophecy gives peace where there is no peace, destiny to a destitute life. After Peter denied Jesus, he went back to fishing. When Jesus found Peter, Peter had been fishing all night long. Laboring in vain! Jesus then leads Peter through a series of questions. I call this 'courting him back'. When Peter was in a place to hear, the Lord began to prophesy to Peter.

John 21:18-19
"Most assuredly, I say to you, when you were younger, you girded yourself and walked where you wished; but when you are old, you will stretch out your hands, and another will gird you and carry you where you do not wish." This He spoke, signifying by what death he would glorify God. And when He had spoken this, He said to him, 'Follow Me.'" **(NKJ)**

A Condition To The Promise

The Lord revealed the future of Peter. I am sure that at this time this word didn't make any sense to Peter, but later it would prove itself to be accurate and a tool of strength in his life. Every prophetic word has conditions on them. The Lord added the final words "FOLLOW ME." Many people would have ignored this command. Yes command, it is not a suggestion it a condition to the word of the Lord coming true. For example, many times the Lord will encourage someone with a word concerning their finances, stating that He desires to bless them.

Let's be very realistic; yes, God wants to bless, but if you're not in covenant with Him, how can He bless you? If you don't pay tithes how can He bypass His written Word of covenant and bless you when the Word says that you rob God and as a result, you will become the recipient of a curse?

I have said to churches prophetically, that if they would continue what they were doing, the Lord was going to bring great increase. The funny thing is most of the people only heard that the Lord was going to bring great increase and stopped doing what the Lord had asked of them, so the increase stopped. The prophetic should remove all second-guessing of whether or not it is going to come to pass, but often it causes more second-guessing when people try to process it with their natural understanding. The Word of the Lord usually challenges all reason.

Later in Peter's life, we see the reason why God spoke the Word. When you receive or give a word, you must understand that it is given for a reason. Either they are in a time that they need to use it for war, or they will soon need it for war.

1 Timothy 1:18-19
"This charge I commit to you, son Timothy, according to the prophecies previously made concerning you, that by them you may wage the good warfare, having faith and a good conscience, which some having rejected, concerning the faith have suffered shipwreck," **(NKJ)**

God gives the prophetic to give us power to wage a good warfare in keeping faith and a good conscience. These are the two things that the devil is trying to take from us. If the devil can take these things from us, then he can cause us to be shipwrecked, and cause us to abort our destiny, to cast away purpose.

The Lord was equipping Peter to fight a good fight in the future. When you speak to people in the Name of the Lord you are equipping them to fight a good fight. Sometimes it is hard for you or the person that you give the word to, to understand why you are giving the word.

Acts 21:10-14
"And as we stayed many days, a certain prophet named Agabus came down from Judea. When he had come to us, he took Paul's belt, bound his own hands and feet, and said, 'Thus says the Holy Spirit, 'So shall the Jews at Jerusalem bind the man who owns this belt, and deliver him into the hands of the Gentiles.' Now when we heard these things, both we and those from that place pleaded with him not to go up to Jerusalem. Then Paul answered, 'What do you mean by weeping and breaking my heart? For I am ready not only to be bound, but also to die at Jerusalem for the name of the Lord Jesus.' So when he would not be persuaded, we ceased, saying, 'The will of the Lord be done.'" **(NKJ)**

Agabus delivered the word of the Lord to Paul regarding the trials that he would come under if he were to go to Jerusalem. I'm sure that Agabus thought that this word would discourage Paul from going, because it described some tough times ahead. Of course if you gave a word like this today, you would be kicked out of many churches and called a heretic without faith. The truth of the matter is, that if he had given any word other than the truth, it would have been in conflict with what God was planning for Paul. Believe it or not, it was the will of God for Paul to go through these trials and that's why the Lord prophesied to him, to encourage him to continue, because God was with him. Remember that the Holy Spirit is in charge of the gifts and He will deliver the right word as long as we keep our agenda out of the way.

When the rest of the company who were with Paul and Agabus heard this word, they immediately tried to convince Paul not to go. A prophetic word is for those times when people around you don't line up with the word of the Lord, and you can with confidence defy all human reasoning and demonic wavering.

Public Prophecy

I once went to a church where the pastor asked me not to speak the prophetic word into the microphone; he preferred me whisper it into the peoples' ears. The reason being that in the past people were harassed by some in his congregation about the time that it was taking for it to come to pass. The truth of the matter is that due season all will see the profiting of the word in God's timing not ours.

There are many reasons why a prophetic minister shouldn't whisper the word into people's ears unless the Holy Spirit leads you to do it that way (usually if it is a rebuke that others need not hear). First, how can the other prophetic ministers test the word, as instructed in 1 Corinthians 14? How can the word be accurately recorded and documented for the times when the person really needs to hear it again? It is scriptural to record the prophetic words, else we would not have many parts of the Old and New Testament. Lastly, if you can't handle people bugging you about the promise, how are you going to overcome the devil when he comes and tells you that it will never come to pass?

How can you be strong, holding on to the word saying; "you shall live and not die", when the doctor comes and says that you have the HIV virus? We have to learn to be tough. If we can be moved by a few people that don't understand what God is saying, then how can we fight when all odds are against us? Agabus was only confirming what the Holy Spirit had been saying in every city that Paul would enter into.

Acts 20:22-24

"And see, now I go bound in the spirit to Jerusalem, not knowing the things that will happen to me there, except that the Holy Spirit testifies in every city, saying that chains and tribulations await me. But none of these things move me; nor do I count my life dear to myself, so that I may finish my race with joy, and the ministry which I received from the Lord Jesus, to testify to the Gospel of the grace of God." **(NKJ)**

The word of the Lord bound Paul in his spirit, strengthened Paul so that nothing could move him from the purpose of God. We can handle the storms of life if we know that God is walking through the storms with us, when we know that God cares enough to warn us of the next season of growth, to prepare us for the following season of promotion. Whether uplifting or warning, when the word of the Lord comes, it should put a faith and good conscience in us. Then we can say the same thing that Paul said, "None of these things move me, I don't count my life dear to myself, but I am willing to do anything to accomplish the mission of the Lord for my life." This confidence is what allowed Peter to fall asleep when he was in jail and Herod threatened his life.

Acts 12:6-9

"And when Herod was about to bring him out, that night Peter was sleeping, bound with two chains between two soldiers; and the guards before the door were keeping the prison. Now behold, an angel of the Lord stood by him, and a light shone in the prison; and he struck Peter on the side and raised him up, saying, 'Arise quickly!' And

his chains fell off his hands. Then the angel said to him, 'Gird yourself and tie on your sandals'; and so he did. And he said to him, 'Put on your garment and follow me.' So he went out and followed him, and did not know that what was done by the angel was real, but thought he was seeing a vision." (NKJ)

Right before our eyes is the fulfillment of Peter's prophecy. Before this time it didn't make much sense. But now it is perfectly clear, Peter was so confident that this couldn't be his day to die because the Lord had already told him how he would die. It wasn't that Peter didn't believe that Herod could kill him, I am sure that the event of James' beheading was enough to confirm the fact that Herod was a serious psychotic lunatic. Also, with two bad smelling guards sleeping next to Peter, it was enough to give him the reality of the situation. With all these things proving that it was going to be the end of his life in less than twenty-four hours, Peter could still fall asleep. I am sure that Peter rehearsed in his mind how the Lord would free him, like most of us when we trust the Lord to deliver us. The Lord is much more creative then we are.

Going back to the word of the Lord. Jesus proclaimed that when Peter was young he would gird himself. We see the first manifestation of the prophetic promise in this passage of scripture when the angel said to him, "Gird yourself and tie on your sandals"; at this point we know that Peter was not to die that morning. There is no clue to the age of Peter, but I assume that he was still young because they didn't carry him where he didn't want to go. Now from this point we can see he was completely delivered. God gives a prophetic word so that we can sleep in the mist of the storm like Jesus did in the boat.

Without getting too deep, I would like to give brief instruction and understanding to the gift of prophecy. First of all, the gift of prophecy has two focal points. The first is corporate (where God will speak through individuals to a body or group of people). The second is individual prophecies (God using an individual to speak to an individual). Going back to the example of me giving an utterance in tongues for the first time and not having the interpretation. I felt hot all over my body, my heart started beating rapidly, my hands became sweaty when the unction of the Lord fell on me to prophesy. This has happened to many of you as you were sitting in church or a Bible study and you didn't have any idea what to do or what was going on. Before I continue I must clarify something, once the tongue is interpreted, the end result is a prophetic word. As soon as the tongue or heavenly language is interpreted, it is transformed into edification.

1 Corinthians 14:5
"I wish you all spoke with tongues, but even more that you prophesied; for he who prophesies is greater than he who speaks with tongues, unless indeed he interprets, that the church may receive edification." **(NKJ)**

I will cover more about the gift of tongues later in this chapter. The one thing that I wanted to make clear is that there is a tongue and interpretation that falls under the category of the gift of prophecy. The Bible clearly states that prophecy is for edification of the church. In context of this scripture, Paul is only referring to the church at this point, not to individual prophetic words. If we will remember that the epistles were written to address certain problem in the apostolic churches, then we will have a better understanding of what was written. Without going into the details of the problem we must understand that Paul was addressing the uses of the corporate gift of prophecy and the corporate gift of tongues and interpretation at the early part of chapter 14 of 1 Corinthians.

Many people will start out using their corporate prophetic gift by sounding the trumpet of tongues beforehand, because they are new to the gift of prophecy. By first speaking the word in tongues, it gives them opportunity to be consumed by the unction of the Holy Spirit until they receive the full prophetic word. Now this doesn't mean that they are speaking in tongues in vain. They are speaking the same message in two different languages. The heavenly, then the earthly language. This is the way the Holy Spirit got me starting to prophesy. I first started off by speaking in tongues and allowing an interpreter to interpret. Then as I gained confidence in the fact that God wanted to use me, the Lord stated giving me the interpretation. This is as scriptural as an interpreter giving the interpretation.

Again in v.5, Paul says, "unless indeed he interprets," describing the person giving the tongue. From this point, I gained confidence and the Lord bypassed the trumpet and gave the direct prophecy. There are times when I will still give the tongue and interpretation or someone else will give the interpretation. So it is not something that is less important, its just that for people starting to be used of God in utterance gifts, it takes the pressure off the rookie and allows someone of more experience to take control.

If you feel like God is trying to get your attention in a service, this is a great way to introduce yourself to operating in the corporate prophetic anointing. Remember, always find out what the protocol of your church is for corporate prophetic words. It will always be more beneficial to you, your pastor and your church, if you submit yourself to the guidance of the leadership. Sometimes it will feel as if you cannot control yourself, but this is not so. You have control of the gift as far as releasing it.

1 Corinthians 14:32
"And the spirits of the prophets are subject to the prophets." **(NKJ)**

I have used and heard this excuse often, "I just couldn't help myself." Or even, "Who are you to stop the word of the Lord?" If this is your response, GROW UP. In the past, I've said this many times and later realized that it was just my ego speaking.

Another way to release a word for the first time, is to write it on a piece of paper and deliver it to the pastor or a leader of the church. I remember when I drove down to California from Washington state, I heard that there was a small church in northern California having a church service, so I stopped by. As soon as I walked in, the Lord gave me a word for that church. So instead of standing up and spouting off, I wrote down the word and gave it to an usher. The usher was so excited that he quickly passed it to the pastor, who immediately stood up and read it. This was exciting even though the congregation didn't know who had received and delivered the word, it just exciting to know that they were blessed. Never go into a new church and start prophesying.

In the church that I am involved in now, the Lord commanded me not to prophecy corporately for the first year. Then after that year, I began to write down whatever God was telling me. There are so many pitfalls to a person being used in a church service. Another is not to ritually prophesy every week in the church service.

People will become familiar with your prophecies and end up missing what God is saying when there is an important word that must be spoken. The prophetic gift is to be protected because we speak in the Name of the Lord. If you prophecy the same thing every week, it's about time for you to go to prayer and get a new word from God or some instruction on how to help the people you are speaking so that you can move into a new revelation!

If you feel the unction to prophecy and another gives the word before you, unless you're adding to the revelation, hold your peace. You will just end up repeating everything that was said, but in a different way. You may think people will understand your version better, but just remain silent and judge the word that was given. If two words have comfort and one is not in line with the others and your word confirms one way or another, then stand and speak forth the word. This is necessary for consistency between the prophetic words. If someone has totally missed it, it would not be Christ-like to get on his or her case. If you have instruction for them, give it another day, today they need to be encouraged to keep on trying.

In 1996, I had the privilege to go to Tanzania to minister to Rwandan refugees in a Tanzanian refugee camp. In this campaign, I taught the ministers in a daytime seminar, and we conducted crusades in the evening. While preaching in a Sunday morning service, the Lord gave a prophecy that the enemy (Satan) was planning for war again and that he was whispering into the ears of the rebel troops to cause them to rise up once more. The first war left many of these ministers without their families and churches. 1.5 million Watusi and Hutu people were slaughtered. So this was a sensitive issue for these people.

To be honest, I didn't think that they would be very happy with the announcement. I thought that they would run me out of their country. But the Lord spoke that He would stop the war short for the sake of the ministers that would pray during this outbreak of war. Then He would send them home to Rwanda in peace and make a nation unified that once had been split in two. Two weeks after the word was spoken, the war broke out in Rwanda and the other refugee camps. But the pastors began to pray. Overnight 100,000 refugees left their war-torn camps, traveling hundreds of miles to come to the only camp that was not experiencing war; the Tanzanian camp! In less than three weeks, they were on their way home in peace. This nation was changed by the prophetic word. God will use whoever is willing to speak, no matter what the danger may be.

Individual words are just as exciting. At first when the Lord is trying to get your attention, you will feel somewhat the same things that you feel when you get a corporate word. That is if you feel anything. I believe that most beginners will feel something because it is such a new experience for your body to be under this heavenly unction. I have covered how to approach people in earlier chapters. The main things are to make sure that you get their permission and if you have their permission to speak to them, not to cast pearls before swine. And don't always expect people to understand everything at that time. Many times in a meeting I will speak to someone about a situation in their life or family and they will have no knowledge of it until they go home and get the news. Often people are so shocked at the fact that God is speaking to them that they can't remember anything. They come up us later and tell us that they remembered who or what we were talking about. Never try to interpret for someone what God is saying to them unless the Lord has for sure shown you what He means. It will cause you trouble as well as the person listening to your advice.

Sometimes, while you are prophesying, you may think to yourself, "what am I saying?" Don't be alarmed, nine out of ten times it is the Lord speaking through you. I remember praying for a young guy about twelve or thirteen years old who had a major back problem. While I was praying for him, the Lord showed me that the boy would be healed within fourteen days, so I spoke this over him and prayed a prayer of agreement. A year later while sitting in a Benny Hinn crusade, this young man's mother came over to me and told me about the miracle that took place in her son's back within the time period that was spoken. But I remember how I felt after the anointing lifted, and I was sitting home rehearsing the different prophetic words and miracles. I thought to myself "What did I say?" After the anointing lifts and you're at home thinking on the course of the day, don't let the devil get you thinking that you missed it before God has a chance to bring it to pass. The worst thing is when a person says that they speak in the Name of the Lord under His unction and then, when the anointing lifts, they change their mind before God can even confirm anything. If you take it back you tie the hands of God.

Most of the time, when you feel like this word is too wild for God, watch out, it just may be God. Another incident, while in Wisconsin in a church service, the Lord showed me a young man that had cancer. God spoke a word to the boy saying this cancer would leave as fast as it came, within six months. Every time his parents would take him to treatment, they would say, "Thank You, Lord that we only have four more months of this to endure," then three months, then two months. How could cancer fight this type of faith in God's prophetic words? Most of us take the prophetic word so lightly. Today this young man is completely healed by the prophetic word: an utterance of miracle working power. Step out of the boat and allow God to use you to edify the Body of Christ.

Diverse Kinds Of Tongues

There are three different uses of the gift of tongues: prophecy, prayer, and the communication of the Gospel. Both prophecy and the communication of the Gospel is God speaking to man His eternal plan. The prayer language is the Holy Spirit making intercession for us and through us, speaking mysteries to God. (1 Corinthians 14:2)

Romans 8:26
"Likewise the Spirit also helps in our weaknesses. For we do not know what we should pray for as we ought, but the Spirit Himself makes intercession for us with groanings which cannot be uttered." **(NKJ)**

The purpose of praying in the heavenly language is to have the ability to intercede and pray with power. We all should have this gift of praying in the heavenly language. Without getting too detailed, I would like to give scriptural references for the need and availability of this prayer language.

Acts 2:38-39
"Then Peter said to them, 'Repent, and let every one of you be baptized in the name of Jesus Christ for the remission of sins; and you shall receive the gift of the Holy Spirit. For the promise is to you and to your children, and to all who are afar off, as many as the Lord our God will call.'" **(NKJ)**

This scripture alone is enough to confirm that God wants every believer to receive the gift of the Holy Spirit. The only people who cannot receive this gift are the ones that Jesus never called, and we know by the scriptures that Jesus called all. All are called! So this promise is for you! It doesn't matter what denomination you belong to. That means Catholic, Lutheran, Presbyterian, Baptist, Pentecostal, or Charismatic. All who confess Jesus must be filled and gifted by the Holy Spirit. Jesus said that we will be filled with the Holy Spirit and then His power will fill us. This is the promise, that we would receive power after the Holy Spirit has come upon us (Acts 1:8). When the unction of the Holy Spirit came upon the disciples, there came an utterance from them and they spoke with other tongues. Let's look at this scripture.

Acts 2:1-4
"Now when the Day of Pentecost had fully come, they were all with one accord in one place. And suddenly there came a sound from heaven, as of a rushing mighty wind, and it filled the whole house where they were sitting. Then there appeared to them divided tongues, as of fire, and one sat upon each of them. And they were all filled with the Holy Spirit and began to speak with other tongues, as the Spirit gave them utterance." **(NKJ)**

The Holy Spirit gave them the utterance. The key to the gift of tongues is that the Holy Spirit gives the utterance. When I first got saved, I was filled with the Holy Spirit and spoke in other tongues. The people praying for me were praying in other tongues over me. As they were praying, I was thinking, "How do I do this, what language will I speak in, maybe I'll speak Arabic." On top of these things going through my head, I was slightly intoxicated with four 16oz. bottles of imported beer. At the time, I was accustomed to having at least two beers with my dinner. So I went to this meeting after having dinner and I was a little buzzed. But after a few minutes of prayer, I stopped listening to them and heard a still small voice (utterance) in my heart. So I repeated what the Holy Spirit was telling me to say.

I hope that this blows away every religious thought that any of you have had about being perfect before you can be filled. Jesus fills you to help you become perfect. When Peter preached to the gentiles in Cornelius' home, they were filled and spoke with tongues and magnified God. In Ephesus, Paul and John laid hands on the disciples and they were filled with the Holy Spirit, spoke in other tongues and prophesied.

After Peter and the disciples left the upper room, men from every nation under the sun were in Jerusalem and heard them speaking in their native tongues. This was an incredible miracle. God reversed the curse that was once sent upon man when man thought that they were self-sufficient enough to build a tower to reach God. God spoke from heaven and confused the tongues of men. At Jesus' death, God brought complete restoration to us by giving us gifts that would return us back to our original state as the sons of God. The Holy Spirit brought the restoration by changing their tongues so that all could understand what God was saying. I believe that in these last days we will find this gift more active in the delivery and reception of the Gospel.

Acts 2:6-11
"And when this sound occurred, the multitude came together, and were confused, because everyone heard them speak in his own language. Then they were all amazed and marveled, saying to one another, "'Look, are not all these who speak Galileans? And how is it that

we hear, each in our own language in which we were born? Parthians and Medes and Elamites, those dwelling in Mesopotamia, Judea and Cappadocia, Pontus and Asia, Phrygia and Pamphylia, Egypt and the parts of Libya adjoining Cyrene, visitors from Rome, both Jews and proselytes, Cretans and Arabs-- we hear them speaking in our own tongues the wonderful works of God.'" (NKJ)

The purpose of this particular use of the gift of tongues is to communicate the Gospel to those that you could not speak to in your natural ability. Many misled people think that this gift is received by natural learning, if this was true, how could it be a gift (endowment) of the Holy Spirit? I know of an elderly woman who had this gift operating in her life. She was taking a cab in a foreign country. She didn't speak the language and she gave the driver instructions on a note. The driver took off and started driving in the wrong direction. As she noticed that he was going the wrong way, she began praying in other tongues, without her knowledge the Holy Spirit began to speak through her to the man in his native language. The man stopped the car and turned around to look at this lady and said in English, "How can you speak my language?" The man fully understood English the whole time, but pretended as if he didn't understand her until the Lord rebuked him.

As she explained that she didn't know his language, but her God did, the man began to cry and tell her what the Lord had said through her. The Holy Spirit rebuked the man for his evil heart and demanded that he would repent and give his life to Jesus. The man was so fearful that he made her leave his cab. This woman was saved through the gift of tongues. As the church truly begins to understand this gift and expect God to move in this way, the nations of the world will open up to the Gospel in a way like never before. Nations can be turned in a day by such a powerful manifestation as the gift of tongues.

Interpretation Of Tongues

A few times, while overseas, I experienced the gift of interpretation of a native tongue. I didn't hear it in my ears, but I understood it in my heart. It wasn't for a long period of time. I believe for the ability to operate in both the gift of interpretation of the native tongue, as well as the ability to speak in other foreign languages by the Spirit of God. On the day of Pentecost, these men heard by the Holy Spirit the message of God. The Holy Spirit initiated this. But when it comes to tongues in prayer and prophecy, we can ask for the interpretation.

1 Corinthians 14:13-14
"Wherefore let him that speaketh in an unknown tongue pray that he may interpret. For if I pray in an unknown tongue, my spirit prayeth, but my understanding is unfruitful." (KJV)

Again this scripture confirms that there is a gift that enables us to pray to God, and unless we have the interpretation, we will not have understanding. For most of us it is good for our spirit to pray without our mind having understanding, so that fear, doubt, and other hindrances that the human mind produces can not keep God from being magnified in our lives. Paul's thought towards this was, why not have both the ability to pray with understanding and the ability to pray without understanding?

Praying without understanding doesn't mean praying in tongues and reading a magazine. It means to pray in tongues and thinking on Jesus, unless the Lord is giving understanding through the gift of interpretation. I remember a time when I was ministering to a young man in my youth ministry and we were praying in tongues. As he was praying, I began to see flashes of his family and his brother in particular was standing out to me. After he finished praying, I told him what he was praying for. He said that his brother was indeed heavy on his heart. This was the interpretation of his tongue or prayer language. Sometimes, when I am praying, I will get the understanding of what the Spirit is praying by visions or the still small voice of the Holy Spirit. Sometimes it is so subtle that I could confuse it with my own conscience. Next time you pray in the spirit, pray that the Lord will give you interpretation of what you are praying for, and then look for subtle intuitions or nudges of the Holy Spirit. After a while of seeking for this, you will begin to recognize how the gift works.

In some of our meetings, the Lord will lead me to have the person that I am ministering to pray by the Spirit. Then the Holy Spirit gives me the interpretation of their prayer and the answer to their prayer.

Interpretation of the gift of tongues that is spoken corporately is very similar to how the prophetic gift operates. But it can only be initiated by the release of the gift of tongues. A person can't give an interpretation unless there is something to be interpreted. I have heard many people say that it is an interpretation verses a translation, but they are straining at gnats by using the English definition of this word. The actual word is hermeneia (her-may-ni'-ah), in the Greek, which means translation. Although this is the meaning of the word, the idea is that it is a translation of purpose and definition, not one of words.

When the utterance in tongues is released, is when the interpreter will start to feel uncomfortable. The palms are sweaty, the heart is beating, heat all over your body (it may feel like an anxiety attack in the beginning). Like I said before, the manifestation of the anointing may not be the same, or you may not even experience any tangible feeling. But God must get your attention somehow to let you know that it is you who must give the interpretation. Just open your mouth and let the revelation go. With the interpretation of tongues and prophecy, you will not receive all of the word at the time of utterance. The Lord will deliver the revelation as you start, so you must always be willing to take a step in faith. Don't worry, God will never let you down.

While you're being used in these gifts, never be ashamed of any mistakes that you might make. This is all part of stepping out. If people give you a hard time and they aren't willing to teach you how to do it properly, most of the time they have never been used of God through that gift.

The Utterance Gifts': Practical Application

Recognition: Recognize these gifts by the desires of your heart. The Lord allows us to have a desire for the things of God and then He leads us and teaches us how to fulfill these desires. Some gifts will be easier to operate in because of your personality, motivational and/or five-fold gifting. These gifts usually have a tangible anointing that will accompany them. You may feel as if you are getting warm all over, as if your breath has instantly become shortened, or you may even feel overwhelmed by the Holy Spirit. To some this feels like an anxiety attack. It is the Holy Spirit getting your attention so that He can show what He desires to do through you. Once you realize what is happening. Clarity will come to you concerning a need or circumstance along with the understanding that you are supposed to speak on the behalf of God. Many of these gifts will be very natural for you to operate in and will occur easily. Another way to recognize these gifts is by analyzing what is happening while you are under the anointing; what is your first thought? Is it to find someone to pray for or is it to prophesy? This will reveal your heart's desire.

Operation: You must always regard the etiquette of the church when operating within the local church setting. Look for the opportune time to release the word, tongue or interpretation (for instance, in between songs, or at a quiet point in the service). For individual words, look for openness and faith on the part of the receiver. Never bombard or overwhelm someone that is not ready to receive. Prophecy will be revelation of an event or need with a promise from God to get involved. It will be edifying, exhorting, and comforting. It can deal with the past, present, or future. There is never condemnation in God's words, but always reveals the love of God. Tongues and interpretation will operate in these same realms. The Holy Spirit is the initiator of these gifts; it called the unction. These three gifts will never operate without His unction, except for when we speak the sure word of prophecy (scripture), which is already inspired and can be initiated by prayer. This is a safe way to step out in faith. If you receive a word and are a little intimidated to give it verbally, write it down and give it to them. This is better than doing nothing. Although the word should best be uttered, this is still effective. Ask God to use you in these three gifts and prepare yourself to jump in and make a difference in someone's life.

Development: An intimate relationship with the Lord is the key to developing the gifts of utterance, because you must know the person on whose behalf you are speaking. You have His heart and intention in mind. Prayer develops this intimacy; reading develops godly personality and accuracy. Obedience is the key to God trusting you and being able to use you whenever He desires. Through obedience you will be used of God and your gift will increase by the reason of your use. The more you give, the more you receive. Challenge yourself and be willing to fail sometimes. Mistakes will not end your ability to be used, nor God's desire to use you. Humbly except your mistake and move on. Ask the Holy Spirit to teach and lead you and you'll be o.k. Pray, read, and obey and your life will change for the better.

"The mandate is set,
the gifts are given,
and the land
is ours to possess."

Chapter Seven

THE FINAL CALL

The Supernatural Church

The entire world is waiting as the end of the twentieth century approaches. The world is preparing to have the greatest party of all times on the last night of 1999. The heavens are anticipating the greatest move of the Holy Spirit that has ever hit the face of the earth. A move that will bring the church into the glory that will fulfill the word of the Lord; that the glory of the latter house would be greater then the former house.

Haggai 2:9
"'The glory of this latter temple shall be greater than the former' says the LORD of hosts. And in this place I will give peace,' says the LORD of hosts.'" **(NKJ)**

But what is the church doing? What are we, as the Temple of God, doing to prepare for the greatest harvest that the World has ever seen? It always seems as if the Church is a full step behind the World. The business world starts to talk about leadership, so the Church begins to get on the fad of leadership. It's true that we needed to learn about leading people, but we, the Church, should be setting the trends. The World talks about being politically correct, the next thing you see is that churches are going to seeker-sensitive services that will not offend the unbeliever. Let me ask you something, could you see Jesus being politically correct to the Pharisees? Instead of calling them children of the devil, maybe He would call them slightly confused persons. The supernatural Church and believer will not follow trends; we will set them. It has been done in history whenever religion was not able to stop what God was trying to do. Rock N' Roll, although the devil has taken it and took it to it's full potential, started in the church.

The establishment of the five-fold ministry will help correct the desire of many who follow after worldly fads. The apostolic and prophetic ministry will help keep fresh input and direction in the Body of Christ. As the five-fold ministry comes into unity, the Church will mature. As the Church matures, Christians will desire to be used in ministering and not just sitting around being fed. Laymen will feel the urgency of these last days and will not want to wait for people to come to a church service to get saved and touched by God. The new millennium believer will walk in the same power that was released to the early Church.

The Church is being setup for a time of favor, which will bring spiritual, physical and financial increase. This will result in the removal of the reproach of the Church that has come from the world because we have not been led by the Holy Spirit, but by presumption and the flesh. This same favor is opening doors for Christians to go into arenas that we have not had access to in the past; film and TV, fashion, politics, sports and education. Not only are these doors being opened but also opportunity for ministry is coming. The same favor that was on Joseph is upon men and women who refuse to be religious, but will never compromise Godliness.

Who Is Called To Be A 'Supernaturalist'?

All are called to be supernaturalists, meaning all are called to be led by the Holy Spirit and rely on the spiritual gifts of the Spirit of God. Joseph was brought before Pharaoh and this generation will stand before great men by the use of their spiritual gifts.

Politicians will give prophetic words behind close doors to other politicians. Fashion models, in the changing room, will be praying for other models that need a touch from God. In all walks of life, the Holy Spirit will be able to use us at any time He desires.

Why is this so difficult for us to us to believe? The psychic hotline brings in over two billion dollars a year. The leading television shows consist of subjects such as aliens, and paranormal events. The devil is trying to distract and confuse people from Kingdom business. Consequently, this is all working for the good to the furthering of the Gospel; it is just stirring interest and desire for true supernatural power. The demand for spiritual equipping is rising in the world and the church. Let the true leaders of the world get in front of the next move that is going to hit this planes. Already corporations are organizing seminars and conventions for eastern meditation, hypnotism, and occult activities. These same corporations are calling in psychics to give spiritual guidance for future business dealings. Even our government has spent 20 million dollars over the last 20 years on psychic advice. That's 1 million dollars a year, this money could be going to missionary work if we would get our act together and believe God to give us the gifts that the world is desiring to find. We must be bold enough to meet the need of this spiritually bankrupt society. For such a time as this, are we entrusted by God to touch this generation! It is incredible how God believes and trusts in us, so much that He has saved us for this space of time.

The mandate is set, the gifts are given, and the land is ours to possess. Our marching orders read, "Soldiers of redemption, possess and occupy all territories!" The objective of a soldier of redemption is to redeem the time, redeem souls, and everything that devil has tried to keep from us; all things that have been lost, stolen or blinded from our eyes. Take it back for you are equipped to do so!

A soldier of redemption is a supernaturalist and must be acquainted with the three P's of Possessing: **Pressure, Passion & Power.**

Pressure

Supernaturalists are people who know how to adjust to pressure. As a Christian, there are many pressures that comes with the lifestyle. Pressures of life, pressures of persecution, pressures of living godly, pressures of spiritual attacks and testing, and pressures of faithfulness. Just as a diamond is formed by pressure, these pressures form us into a precious gem for the Kingdom of God.

We as supernaturalists will learn to appreciate these seasons of pressure, knowing that momentary affliction cannot be compared with the glory that shall be revealed in us.

Deep-sea divers rely on the engineer on the ship above, on the surface of the ocean. As the diver dives into the deep, dark abyss, he must be careful to have a light to see and pressure meters available. The light is for when he gets too deep to see what is in front of him, he can illuminate his way with this light. The deeper he goes, the darker it will become. The engineer in the ship above must regulate the pressure of the diving suit according to the pressure that is coming against him the deeper he goes. If, for whatever reason, his suit fails to adjust to this precise pressure, it would cause him to implode. The inward pressure must be the same or more as the outward pressures.

Each day there are people who go through this implosion, suicide, nervous breakdowns, mental illness, depression and oppression. These are just a few ways that implosion manifests in lives when people don't know how to adjust to the pressures of life. Spiritual deficiencies cause emotional and physical breakdown.

Being supernatural is not being weirdo freaks that always seem as if they are living on cloud nine. Being supernatural is learning how to apply the mind of Christ in every environment of life, imparting instead of drawing, and walking in the power of the resurrected King in every opportunity. As supernatural people go through pressures, they find a light in the time of darkness. Looking in the Word, waiting for the word of the Lord, knowing that as soon as the word comes, faith rises and doubt flees, angels come and the devil leaves. The Word brings illumination, David exclaimed that at the entrance of God's Word brings light and understanding. This is what the devil hates, men and women of God that trust in the Word of the Lord. God's light will illuminate any abyss we find ourselves in.

Each time that I have gone through a trial, I found peace in the Word of God, holding onto any scripture that would fit into my circumstances. I felt that at any time, I could sink if I let go of His Word, but as long as I held on I would be okay. With every one of these trials, I heard the voice of God right before the trial was finished. As soon as I heard His voice, I held onto the written and the spoken Word. The devil was in trouble! Your soul will be anchored in the Word of the Lord and the enemy can't blind you any longer.

Fortunately, the engineer above, in our ship of life, is our diving buddy and knows what is going on in our life and can encourage us as we walk. There is no better prayer partner than the Holy Spirit, when we don't feel like praying or if we don't know how to pray, He prays with and for us. As we pray in the Spirit, we build up our most holy faith. Building our spirit-man within these diving suits, so that we can withstand the pressures of life. When you find yourself under pressures, you should find yourself praying in the Spirit even more than usual. This will result in your inward strength to balance out the outward pressure. The enemy hates this as well, because instead of having a tizzy fit at the times that you would normally loose your cool, you walk through with faith that cannot be moved. Overcoming all doubt, fear, and unbelief!

Passion

This faith will result in vision; vision will result in passion. Every person has some type of passion, but of course not all passion is progressive. My Pastor says that a person can find their passion through analyzing "what makes them tick or what makes them ticked." Passion is an emotion that fuels action toward a set vision. Anger, fear, frustration, lust, pride, and love are all forms of passion. Each one of these emotions forms an outlook on a vision. Young people in the ghetto find themselves forming a vision of escaping the bondage of poverty and lack, because of the anger that has been formed from not having what they need. Children from broken families make up their minds that they will do whatever it takes to have a good and healthy marriage. These passions are formed through hardships, but they can still create progressive passions. Passions for transformation instead of conformation; 'Supernaturalists' will learn to take the difficulties and disappointments of pressure and turn it into progressive passion. Once the passion is in play, then the person of passion will be consumed with ideas of making these visions come to pass. First comes pressure, then vision, then faith and hope, then action; keeping passion progressive instead of destructive. Hitler had passion, but his passion didn't care about who he walked over or hurt. His passion was ungodly, and not for the betterment of mankind, nor the Kingdom of God. The whole idea of this is that the men and women of God must have a passion that will make them willing to do whatever it takes to further the Kingdom of God.

The prophetic ministry is here to help us harness our passion to the highest productivity. If a person has vision and passion toward their purpose, then they will go through every obstacle and jump any hurdle to reach that goal. The word of the Lord is like the finish line to a hurdler. A hurdler doesn't focus on the hurdles that are in front of him, his eyes are always on the string at the finish line. Actually, an accomplished hurdler will know exactly how many steps there are between each hurdle so that he will never have to look anywhere other that the finish line. Supernatural people will not have to worry about the steps to the vision because they know that their steps are ordered of the Lord. They are already set! Keep godly passion and know that the Lord has everything else taken care of.

Power

The Lord has never given anyone a purpose and then withheld the power from him or her needed to accomplish what was set before him or her. We are empowered to fulfill the vision that is set before us. We are getting close to the end and the closer we get, the greater the fight is, but the truth of the matter is that this generation will never be happy unless they are fighting. No other generation has ever had to go through what this generation is called to go through. On the other hand, there has never been a generation that has been so empowered like this generation. We are empowered, technologically, and intelligently; more equipped than any other peoples to take this world.

The Lord has saved the best for last and empowered us for this last day! This is the reason many of us are so dissatisfied; we have a sense of greatness but don't understand it. We tend to blame this dissatisfaction on our jobs, marriages, families, or lack of material gain. The truth is that these frustrations are from a divine dissatisfaction upon a warring generation. Warriors are not happy unless they are in war. Joshua's generation was formed for war. Their purpose was to take the children of God into the Promised Land; overcoming the enemies that possessed the land. Just as they were empowered to possess, so are we empowered to possess!

Prepare for possession!

GIFTS TEST

1) Which of the following are the strongest two desires?
__a) To help people that are hurting.
__b) To have understanding.
__c) To know the details of circumstances.
__d) To believe for the impossible.
__e) To give people answers and understanding.
__f) To give instruction on how to solve problems.
__g) The ability to supernaturally communicate
       God's Word in foreign languages.
__h) The ability to breakdown communication problems.
__i) To follow instructions that will create a dramatic
change.

**2) If you see a young man/woman sitting on the side of
the road, with their face in their hands as if they were
in need, what would be your first thought?**
__a) They must be in pain; spiritually, emotionally or
       physically.
__b) I wonder what the circumstances are in their life?
__c) I wonder what God has to say to this young
       man/woman?

3) If you have a chance to minister to him/her, what would you do?

__a) Ask if he/she needed prayer or if you could pray for him/her.

__b) Sit next to him/her and begin communication, waiting for an opportunity to minister.

__c) Intercede from a distance then approach him/her when you're sure of what to do.

__e) Walk on.

4) What is most important to you?

__a) Hearing from God.

__b) Seeing God's power.

__c) Speaking on God's behalf.

5) Based upon the definitions of the gifts of the Spirit in this book, which of the following two gifts do you find most life changing?

__a) The gifts of healings

__b) The gift of prophecy

__c) The gift of word of knowledge

__d) The gift of discerning of spirits

__e) The gift of word of wisdom

__f) The gift of tongues

__g) The gift of interpretation

__h) The gift of faith

__i) The gift of working of miracles

NOTES

1. Which of the following are the strongest two desires?

a) The gift of healings
b) The gift of discerning of spirits
c) The gift of word of knowledge
d) The gift of faith
e) The gift of prophecy
f) The gift of word of wisdom
g) The gift of tongues
h) The gift of interpretation
i) The gift of the working of miracles

2. If you see a young man or woman sitting on the side of the road, with their face in their hands as if they were in need, what would be your first thought?

a) The gifts of power
b) The gifts of revelation
c) The gifts of utterance

3. If you have a chance to minister to him/her, what would you do?

a) The gifts of power
b) The gifts of revelation
c) The gifts of utterance
d) Carelessness

4. What is most important to you?

a) The gifts of revelation
b) The gifts of power
c) The gifts of utterance